BRITISH GENEALOGICAL PERIODICALS

A BIBLIOGRAPHY OF THEIR CONTENTS

SUPPLEMENT 1

BRITISH GENEALOGY
IN
MISCELLANEOUS JOURNALS

by

Stuart A. Raymond

S.A. & M.J. RAYMOND
GENEALOGICAL BIBLIOGRAPHERS

Published by
S.A. & M.J. Raymond
6 Russet Avenue
Exeter
Devon U.K.
EX1 3QB

First published 1994

Cataloguing in publication data:

RAYMOND, Stuart A., 1945- *British genealogical periodicals:
a bibliography of their contents, Supplement 1. British genealogy
in miscellaneous journals.* British genealogical bibliographies.
Exeter: S.A. & M.J. Raymond, 1994.

DDC: 016.9291

ISBN 0-9588144-4-9

ISSN: 1033-2065

Produced for the Publishers by
Robert Boyd, Printing & Publishing Services,
260 Colwell Drive, Witney, Oxfordshire OX8 7LW

Contents

Cover illustration:

North Molton Church

Reproduced by courtesy of
West Country Studies Library

Introduction

This bibliography lists the genealogical contents of six important national and regional archaeological and antiquarian journals, and thus complements the contents listings of genealogical journals to be found in the other volumes of *British genealogical periodicals*. Archaeology is a term which had a much wider connotation in the nineteenth century than it has today; it encompassed a wide range of historical disciplines. Consequently, there are many articles of genealogical relevance in the major archaeological journals which commenced publication before 1900. Contributions to the major regional antiquarian journals also contain many valuable genealogical works. The lack of adequate contents listings has meant that only the most persistent and experienced genealogists are likely to be able to identify those items which may be of relevance. The present bibliography has been compiled in the hope of creating greater awareness of a valuable resource.

The six journals covered in this work, with the abbreviations used to identify them, are:

A.A.S.R.P.   *Reports and papers of the Associated Architectural Societies.* 40 vols. 1850-1930. Continued by: *Reports and papers of the architectural and archaeological societies of the counties of Lincoln and Northampton.* 2 vols (numbered 41-2), 1934-7.

Arch.   *Archaeologia: or, miscellaneous tracts relating to antiquity.* London: Society of Antiquaries of London, 1773-

A.J.   *Archaeological journal.* London: Royal Archaeological Institute of Great Britain and Ireland, 1844-

J.B.A.A.   *Journal of the British Archaeological Association.* London: the Association, 1845-94. New series, 1895-1936. 3rd series. 1937-

N.G.   *Northern genealogist.* 6 vols. York: John Sampson, 1895-1903.

Reliquary.   *The Reliquary, quarterly journal and review: a depository for precious relics – legendary, biographical and historical, illustrative of the habits, customs and pursuits of our forefathers.* 26 vols. London: John Russell Smith; Derby: Bemrose & Sons, 1860-86. New series, London: Bemrose & Sons, 1888-94. Continued as: *The Reliquary and illustrated archaeologist: a quarterly journal and review.* 8 vols. London: Bemrose & Sons, 1895-1902.

These particular titles are amongst the most important national and regional antiquarian and archaeological journals carrying genealogical contributions; the regional titles cover much wider areas than other similar journals. The *Reliquary* claimed to be a national journal, although in practice it had a strong bias towards the North, and particularly towards Derbyshire and adjacent counties. Member societies of the Associated Architectural Societies were drawn from the region between Yorkshire, Bedfordshire and Worcestershire, whilst the *Northern genealogist* attracted contributions relating to the region between Ely and the Scottish border. The contents of the latter are listed here almost in their entirety; only brief notes and queries, news items, and short reviews are excluded.

The criteria used in selecting articles for inclusion has been whether they include information likely to be of direct value to genealogical research. Usefulness, rather than comprehensiveness, has determined the material to be included. Further information on the selection of material is provided in the text where necessary. Citations are arranged in subject order, sub-divided, where appropriate, by place and family name. Indexes to authors, places, and family names are provided. Works which have not been listed here may be identified by using the published indexes, which are available as follows:

Archaeologia
An index to the Archaeologia ... from volume I to volume L inclusive ... London: Society of Antiquaries of London, 1889.

Archaeologia ... index to volumes 51-100 (second series, volumes 1-50). London: Society of Antiquaries, 1970.

Antiquaries Journal
DALLAS, V. M. *The Antiquaries journal ... general index, volumes 1-X.* London: Oxford University Press, 1934.

NISBET, DAPHNE. *The Antiquaries journal ... general index, volumes XI-XX.* London: Oxford University Press, 1976.

PROCTER, PHOEBE. *The Antiquaries journal ... general index, volumes XXI-XXX.* London: Oxford University Press, 1971.

The Antiquaries journal ... general index, volumes XXXI-XL. London: Oxford University Press, 1971.

The Antiquaries journal ... general index, volumes XLI-L. London: Oxford University Press, 1978.

Journal of the British Archaeological Association
BIRCH, WALTER DE GRAY. *The Journal of the British Archaeological Association: general index to volumes 1-XXX.* London: the Association, 1875.

BIRCH, WALTER DE GRAY. *The Journal of the British Archaeological Association: general index to volumes XXXI to XLII, the Collectanea archaeologica, Vols. I, II, and the separate volumes for the Winchester and Gloucester congresses.* London: the Association, 1887.

ROOK, F. FERRARD. *The Journal of the British Archaeological Association: general index to volumes XLIII to LII, 1887-1896.* London: the Association, 1915.

AUSTIN, ROLAND. *The Journal of the British Archaeological Association: general index to new series, volumes I-XXV (1895-1919) ...* London: the Association, 1924.

Reports and papers of the Associated Architectural Societies
FOSTER, C. W., & DUDDING, R.C. *An index to volumes I-XXXVI of Reports and papers of the Associated Architectural Societies.* Lincoln: Lincolnshire Chronicle, 1929. More detailed indexes are available for vols.1-8, 9-14, 15-19 and 20-25.

Reliquary
RIDEN, PHILIP. *An index to the Reliquary first series, volumes 1-26, 1860-86.* Occasional paper 2. Matlock: Derbyshire Record Society, 1979.

This work is intended to complement my *English genealogy: an introductory bibliography*, and the other works in the *British genealogical bibliographies* series. It is hoped to compile separate genealogical bibliographies for each county, and in due course many of the works cited here will also be cited in the various county volumes. This project is unlikely to be completed for a number of years; in the meantime, genealogists, historians and librarians will all find the present work a useful aid in their research.

Once again, I would like to thank the librarians of those institutions whose collections I have consulted. Most of the work for this volume was done at Exeter University Library and the Bodleian Library, Oxford, with occasional forays to the Devon and Exeter Institution, Exeter Public Library, Leeds Public Library, and the Somerset Archaeological and Natural History Society's library at Taunton Castle. Thanks are due to Bob Boyd, who has seen this volume through the press, and to Jeremy Gibson, for his support. My thanks also to my good friends John and Freda Cammack, in whose home I was a guest whilst I worked in Oxford. Finally, my thanks are due to my wife and children, who have learnt to live with **British Genealogical Bibliographies**.

Stuart A. Raymond

1. PARISH REGISTERS AND OTHER RECORDS OF BIRTHS MARRIAGES AND DEATHS

It should be noted that few of the articles listed here are full transcripts of parish registers. Most have some extracts, although a few are merely discussions.

'Waifs and strays', *N.G.* **1**, 1895, 156-8 & 240-44; **2**, 1896, 31-3, 67-9 & 135-8; **3**, 1900, 138-9; **4**, 1901, 17, 67 & 139; **5**, 1902, 12, 99 & 129.

Berkshire

Newbury
MONEY, WALTER. 'Notes to the parish registers of Newbury', *J.B.A.A.* N.S. **1**, 1895, 157-83. Notes common surnames; general discussion.

Cambridgeshire
'Ely marriage licences', *N.G.* **1**, 1895, 15-19 & 73-8. In continuation of Gibbon's *Ely episcopal records*. Covers 1582-91.
'Some marriage licences, ordination entries, &c., at Ely', *N.G.* **1**, 1895, 206-10. 16-18th c.

Thorney
EGAR, S. 'Thorney and its registers', *Reliquary* **12**, 18712, 143-44. Includes a few extracts, 17-18th c.

Cumberland
HOWE, JOHN J. 'Carlisle marriage bonds', *N.G.* **1**, 1895, 105, 143 & 222; **2**, 1896, 7, 109-10 & 185-6; **3**, 1900, 40 & 80; **4**, 1901, 37-8. 1700-1737.

Derbyshire
JACKSON, CHARLES. 'The ms. memoranda of George Mower of Barley Woodseats, Co. Derby, *Reliquary* **21**, 1880-81, 107-12 & 215-21; **22**, 1881-2, 92-6. Gives many notices of deaths, etc., in Derbyshire and adjacent counties, 17-18th c.
JEWITT, LLEWELLYN. 'Funeral certificates of some Derbyshire families, with illustrative notes', *Reliquary* **26**, 1885-6, 150-55 & 187-93. *See also* Sussex. Horsham.

Alvaston
POOLE, E. 'Notes on the parish register and other documents relating to Alvaston, Derbyshire', *Reliquary* **3**, 1862-3, 134-42. Includes a few extracts, 1614-1774.

Ashburne
JOURDAINE, FRANCIS. 'The parish registers of Ashburne, Co. Derby', *Reliquary* **25**, 1884-5, 177-80 & 241-6; **26**, 1885-6, 42-8, 69-72 & 156-60. 16th c.

Ashford in the Water
See Great Longsdon

Bakewell
BELL, W.R. 'An account of the oldest parish registers of Bakewell, Derbyshire', *Reliquary* **5**, 1864-5, 73-79. Includes 17th c. extracts.

Beeley
BELL, W.R. 'Extracts from the oldest parish registers of Beeley, Derbyshire', *Reliquary* **5**, 1864-5, 143-7. 17th c.

Chapel en le Frith
KIRKE, HENRY. 'On the parish registers of Chapel-en-le-Frith', *Reliquary* **6**, 1865-6, 65-8 & 226-32. 17-18th c.

Chesterfield
BRADLEY, FREDERICK. 'The first volume of the register of Chesterfield parish church', *Reliquary* **8**, 1867-8, 9-19. Includes many extracts.

Derby
BERESFORD, W. 'St Alkmund's, Derby, and its oldest parish register', *Reliquary* **10**, 1869-70, 193-202; **11**, 1870-71, 109-14 & 135-40; **12**, 1871-2, 9-13. Includes extracts relating to ministers, and to the families of Gisburne, Parker, Lister, Goodwyn, Bates, Bullocks, Sacheverel, Degge, Hope, Wilmot, Batt, Turner, Holden, Adderley, Sanders (including pedigree), Wright, Burton, Sykes, Alsop, Cockayne, Bage, Woolley, Hodgkinson, etc. For Alsop, see also **12**, 1871-2, 127-8.
REED, S.T. 'On old church registers and other records', *J.B.A.A.* **7**, 1851, 289-303. Brief notes on the registers of St. Alkmund and All Hallows, Derby.

Duffield
'Desultory cuttings from the parish registers of Duffield in the county of Derby', *Reliquary* **23**, 1882-3, 104-6. 17th c.

Eyam
WOOD, WILLIAM. 'A note on the parish register of the church of St Helens, Eyam', *Reliquary* 3, 1862-3, 49-51. Includes a few extracts.

Fenny Bentley
SLEIGH, JOHN. 'Extracts from the parish register of Fenny-Bentley, in the county of Derby', *Reliquary* 7, 1866-7, 104-8.

Great Longsdon
SLEIGH, JOHN. 'Extracts from the parish registers of S. Giles, Great Longsdon, and Holy Trinity, Ashford-in-the-Water', *Reliquary* 2, 1861-2, 155-8.

Hathersage
JOURDAINE, FRANCIS. 'The parish registers of Hathersage', *Reliquary* 10, 1869-70, 164-6 & 239-40. Full transcript, 1627-30.

Marston Montgomery
CLARK, JOHN HALDENBY. 'Notes from the parish registers of Marston Montgomery, County of Derby', *Reliquary* 7, 1866-7, 140-5. Includes many extracts.

Monyash
SLEIGH, JOHN. 'Extracts from the parish registers of Monyash and Taddington, Derbyshire', *Reliquary* 5, 1864-5, 85-8.

Normanton
HOPE, W. 'Extracts from parish registers relating to Normanton families', *Reliquary* 2, 1861-2, 6-10. Extracts from 1560 to 1690.

North Winfield
COX, J. CHARLES. 'Extracts from the parish registers of the parish of North Winfield', *Reliquary* 13, 1872-3, 35-9 & 108-11. 16-17th c.

Somersal Herbert
FITZHERBERT, REGINALD H.C. 'Somersal-Herbert church registers', *Reliquary* 14, 1873-4, 79-80. Includes a transcript of the first page of the register, 1537-50.

Stretton-en-le-Field
FALKNER, T. FELTON. 'The parish register of Stretton-en-le-Field, Co. Derby', *Reliquary* 15, 1874-5, 95-6. Includes a few extracts only.

Taddington
See Monyash.

Tideswell
BAGSHAWE, BENJAMIN. 'Extracts from the parish registers of Tideswell, in the county of Derby', *Reliquary* 8, 1867-8, 209-16.

Wormhill
SLEIGH, JOHN. 'Extracts from the parish registers of Wormhill, in the High Peak', *Reliquary* 4, 1863-4, 237-40.

Youlgreave
SLEIGH, JOHN. 'Extracts from the parish registers of Youlgreave in the county of Derby', *Reliquary* 4, 1863-4, 186-95. See also 5, 1864-5, 54. Also includes extracts from churchwardens' accounts, etc.

Dorset

Cattistock
COLLETT, E. 'The registers of the parish of Cattistock, Co. Dorset', *Reliquary* 26, 1885-6, 137-44 & 222-4. 16-18th c. extracts.

Co. Durham

HOWE, JOHN J. 'Durham marriage bonds', *N.G.* 1, 1895, 54, 106-7, 144-5 & 223-4; 2, 1896, 6, 45-6 & 108-9; 3, 1900, 39-40 & 79-80; 4, 1901, 37. 1662-6.

Essex

Stock Harvard and Ramsden Bellhouse
GIBSON, E.P. 'The parish registers of Stock Harvard cum Ramsden Bellhouse, Essex', *A.J.* 37, 1880, 406-16. Includes extracts.

Hampshire

Newport
ANDREWS, S. 'Note on the parish register of Newport, Isle of Wight', *J.B.A.A.* N.S. 22, 1916, 81-4. General description of the registers.

Kent

Canterbury. Westgate, Holy Cross
See Northamptonshire. Peterborough.

Lancashire

Padiham
FISHWICK, MAJOR. 'Extracts from the registers of the parochial chapel of Padiham, in the county of Lancaster', *Reliquary* 12, 1871-2, 101-5.

Stretford

BAILEY, JOHN EGLINGTON. 'The parish registers of the chapelry of Stretford, near Manchester', *Reliquary* 17, 1876-7, 45-8 & 93-6.

Leicestershire

HARTOPP, HENRY. 'Leicester marriage licences: an abstract of marriage bonds and allegation books preserved in the registry of the archdeaconry of Leicester, 1570-1729', *A.A.S.R.P.* 27(2), 1904, 525-622; 28(1), 1905, 221-332; 28(2), 1906, 663-774; 29(1), 1907, 183-279; 29(2), 1908, 535-84.

Appleby Magna

FALKNER, T. FELTON. 'The parish registers of Appleby Magna', *Reliquary* 12, 1871-2, 139-43. Includes a few extracts, 17-18th c.

Barrow

EDWARDS, J. 'Notes on the parish registers of Barrow and Twyford', *Reliquary* N.S. 1, 1860-61, 231-5. Includes some extracts.

Houghton on the Hill

WINCKLEY, S.T. 'Parish registers of Houghton-on-the-Hill, Co. Leicester, 1582-1639', *A.A.S.R.P.* 25(2), 1900, 419-30.

Loughborough

FLETCHER, W.G. DIMOCK. 'The parish registers of Loughborough, in the county of Leicester', *Reliquary* 13, 1872-3, 194-201. Includes extracts, 16-19th c.

Misterton

BRADBROOK, W. 'Extracts from and notes on the parish registers of Misterton, Co. Leicester', *A.A.S.R.P.* 26(2), 1902, 449-57.

Ratby

HARTOPP, HENRY. 'Parish registers of Ratby, Co. Leicester, 1695-1710', *A.A.S.R.P.* 25(2), 1900, 405-18.

Stanford

SANDON, W.H. 'Stanford church and its registers, &c', *A.A.S.R.P.* 17(1), 1883, 121-53. Includes many extracts, especially relating to Cave family, and to local clergy, also pedigree of Cave, 15-17th c.

Twyford

See Barrow.

Lincolnshire

'Lincoln marriage licences', *N.G.* 1, 1895, 25-32, 97-102, 171-3 & 251-4; 2, 1896, 72-5, 124-7 & 164-7; 3, 1900, 9-12 & 63-71; 4, 1901, 76-81 & 140-45; 5, 1902, 35-44, 90-93 & 144-52; 6, 1903, 7-13 & 81-5. Alphabetical continuation of Gibbon's *Lincoln marriage licences*; incomplete (reached Rownthwaite) when *N.G.* ceased publication.

Kelstern

'Kelstern (Co. Lincoln): transcripts of the parish register', *N.G.* 6, 1903, 90-92. 1562-90.

Kingerby

'Kingerby parish register, Co. Lincoln', *N.G.* 1, 1895, 57-61, 115-20, 180-6 & 216-8. Bishops' transcripts, 1562-1764.

Kirton in Lindsey

HOWLETT, ENGLAND. 'Burial in woollen', *Reliquary* N.S. 5, 1891, 205-8. Includes affidavits from Kirton in Lindsey.

Stamford. St. George

SIMPSON, JUSTIN. 'Extracts from the parish registers of St. George's, Stamford', *Reliquary* 8, 1867-8, 89-96, 151-60 & 216-23.

Stamford. St. John

SIMPSON, JUSTIN. 'Extracts from the parish registers of St. John's, Stamford', *Reliquary* 20, 1879-80, 238-40; 21, 1880-81, 77-80, 157-60 & 222-4; 22, 1881-2, 53-6 & 113-8; 24, 1883-4, 73-80. Includes many biographical notices.

Stamford. St. Martin

SIMPSON, JUSTIN. 'Extracts from the parish registers of St. Martins, Stamford', *Reliquary* 12, 1871-2, 51-5 & 116; 13, 1872-3, 165-70 & 236-42. Includes many genealogical and biographical notes.

Stamford. St. Mary

SIMPSON, JUSTIN. 'Extracts from the parish registers of St. Marys, Stamford', *Reliquary* 9, 1868-9, 113-9; 10, 1869-70, 47-50; 11, 1870-71, 23-6 & 173-6.

Stamford. St. Michael

SIMPSON, JUSTIN. 'Extracts from the parish registers of St. Michaels, Stamford', *Reliquary* 14, 1873-4, 41-6, 74-8 & 231-4; 15, 1874-5, 39-42, 91-4 & 170-4; 16, 1875-6, 45-8, 75-80 & 225-28; 17, 1876-7, 88-92, 202-8;

18, 1877-8, 95-6, 149-52 & 212-6; **19**, 1878-9, 46-8, 107-12 & 166-8; **20**, 1879-80, 117-9. 16-18th c., includes many biographical and genealogical notes.

London and Middlesex

Paul's Wharf
NOBLE, MARK. 'Extracts from the parish register of St Bennet's, St. Paul's Wharf, London', *Arch.* 13, 1800, 274-9. Includes extracts related to the aristocracy only.

Northamptonshire

ELLIOTT, H.L. 'The parish registers of Northampton and the neighbourhood', *A.A.R.S.P.* 6(2), 1862, 200-19. Includes list of surviving registers as in 1862, plus a few extracts.

Clay Coton
POOLE, GORDON H. 'Parish register of Clay Coton, Northants', *N.G.* 2, 1896, 120-3 & 191-4; 3, 1900, 29-32, 92-5 & 140-43; 4, 1901, 13-17. 1541-1614.

Peterborough
'Parish register of St John the Baptist, Peterborough, and Holy Cross, Westgate, Canterbury', *Reliquary* 26, 185-6, 83-5. 16-17th c.

Nottinghamshire

Attenborough
COLLETT, E. 'The old registers of the parish of Attenborough-cum-Bramcote, Nottinghamshire, with extracts and notes', *Reliquary* 12, 1871-2, 33-40 & 105-9; 13, 1872-3, 75-80. Includes list of churchwardens, 1598-1641 and of ministers, 1566-1871, etc.

Bramcote
See Attenborough.

East Retford
COLLETT, E. 'Notes on the old registers of the parish of St. Swithun, East Retford, Nottinghamshire, with extracts', *Reliquary* 16, 1875-76, 217-9; 17, 1876-7, 41-4 & 109-11.

Lenton
LOWE, A.E. LAWSON. 'The parish registers of Lenton in the county of Nottingham', *Reliquary* 13, 1872-3, 11-14. Includes extracts, 16-18th c.

Newark
'Newark-on-Trent parish register: a note of all the marriages from 1650 to 1662', *N.G.* 1, 1895, 46-8.
'Newark parish register', *N.G.* 2, 1896, 157-9. Baptisms and burials, 1650-1.

Rutland

Glaston
SIMPSON, JUSTIN. 'Extracts from the parish registers of Glaston, Co. Rutland', *Reliquary* 25, 1884-5, 43-8, 91-6, 154-60 & 217-20. 16-18th c., includes many biographical notices.
SIMPSON, JUSTIN. 'Additional notes upon the parish registers of Glaston, County Rutland', *Reliquary* 26, 1885-6, 7-12.

Shropshire

Baschurch
LEIGHTON, W.A. 'On Baschurch, County of Salop, and its registers', *Reliquary* 6, 1865-6, 17-28. Includes pedigrees of Clive and Bather, with a list of vicars and many extracts.

Staffordshire

Grindon
SLEIGH, JOHN. 'Extracts from the Grindon registers', *Reliquary* 5, 1864-5, 21-3.

Ipstones
SLEIGH, JOHN. 'Ipstones, Co. Stafford, parish registers', *Reliquary* 9, 1868-9, 256. Extracts, 1562-1708.

Leek
SLEIGH, JOHN. 'Extracts from the parish registers and churchwardens' accounts of the parish of Leek', *Reliquary* 3, 1862-3, 211-17.

Surrey

Mitcham
RICE, ROBERT GARRAWAY. 'On the parish registers of Ss. Peter and Paul, Mitcham, Surrey (from A.D. 1563 to 1679)', *Reliquary* 18, 1877-8, 1-12 & 136-44; 19, 1878-9, 17-23 & 231-6; 20, 1879-80, 44-8. Not completed; to 1597 only. Includes many biographical notes.

Walton on the Hill
MARSHALL, GEORGE W. 'Church notes from Walton-on-the-Hill, Co. Surrey', *Reliquary* 10, 1869-70, 203-5. Includes extracts from parish registers and monumental inscriptions.

Sussex

Clapham
GROVER, J.W. 'Notes on old Clapham registers and parish documents', *J.B.A.A.* **41**, 1885, 299-306. Brief note, including a handful of extracts from the registers.

Horsham
RICE, ROBERT GARRAWAY. 'The Derbyshire militia at Horsham, Sussex, in 1797', *Reliquary* **19**, 1878-9, 128. Parish register extracts and monumental inscriptions.

Worcestershire

Bengeworth
SHAWCROSS, J.P. 'Parish registers of Bengeworth', *A.A.S.R.P.* **6**(1), 1921, 117-26. Includes a few extracts.

Eastham
MARSHALL, GEORGE W. 'Extracts from the parish registers of Eastham, Co. Worcester', *Reliquary* **23**, 1882-3, 220-2; **24**, 1883-4, 45-6. 16-19th c.

Yorkshire
G., A. 'Archbishops' transcripts of parish registers at York', *N.G.* **5**, 1902, 76-7. Brief note.

HOWE, JOHN J. 'Allertonshire marriage bonds', *N.G.* **1**, 1895, 105-6, 143-4 & 222-3; **2**, 1896, 7-8, 46-7, 110 & 186; **3**, 1900, 40 & 81; **4**, 1901, 38. 1730-62.

WHYTEHEAD, T.B. 'Marriage bonds of the Dean and Chapter of York', *N.G.* **2**, 1896, 177-80; **3**, 1900, 33-6, 96-101 & 154-9; **4**, 1901, 28-33, 68-75 & 147-9; **5**, 1902, 47-52, 78-87 & 136-43. 16-19th c.

'Notes on the Quakers' registers at York', *N.G.* **1**, 1895, 245.

'York marriage bonds', *N.G.* **2**, 1896, 27-30, 63-66 & 114-7. 18th c.

Dent
KENDALL, WM. CLEMENT. 'Notes from the parish register of Dent', *N.G.* **5**, 1902, 88-9. Brief extracts.

Drypool
BOULTER, W. CONSITT. 'Some extracts from the parish registers of Drypool, in the East Riding of Yorkshire', *Reliquary* **10**, 1869-70, 54-9; **11**, 1870-71, 88-91. 1572-1803.

Givendale
'Givendale register transcripts', *N.G.* **3**, 1900, 130-31. 1699-1710.

Pickering
See Pocklington.

Pocklington
WHYTEHEAD, T.B. 'Marriage bonds of the peculiar jurisdiction of the Deanery of York', *N.G.* **6**, 1903, 69-73. 1764-9. Pocklington and Pickering area.

Sandal Magna
'Sandal Magna parish register', *N.G.* **3**, 1900, 160-8; **4**, 1901, 52-6 & 81-4. Bishops transcripts, 1598-1631 (not all).

Startforth
BULLEN, MARK W. 'Startforth parish register, Co. York', *N.G.* **2**, 1896, 89-96 & 143-52; **3**, 1900, 54-6, 105-8 & 150-53. 1665-1700.

York. All Saints, Pavement
'The parish register of All Saints, Pavement, York: marriages 1555-1690', *N.G.* **6**, 1903, 64-8. 1555-1611.

York. Holy Trinity, Goodramgate.
'Naval and military notes: parish registers of Holy Trinity, Goodramgate, York', *N.G.* **2**, 1896, 49-52 & 111-3. Extracts of baptisms and burials, 1640-1799; also includes wills of Joshua Guest, 1746, Sarah Guest of Hanover Square, Middlesex, 1749, John Walters, 1643, Richard Watson, 1784 and Joseph Crowe of Portsea, Hampshire, 1783.

York. St Maurice
'Marriage registers of St. Maurice, York (a complete abstract)', *N.G.* **3**, 1900, 181-4; **4**, 1901, 39-41 & 88-92; **5**, 1902, 96-8. 1648-1812.

13

2. MONUMENTAL INSCRIPTIONS

Many inscriptions were printed in the six journals covered by this bibliography. This listing is not comprehensive; rather, it includes only those works likely to be of genealogical value. There are many articles dealing with the art and archaeology of memorials, but which give little genealogical information; these are excluded. When consulting the articles listed here, remember that they do not necessarily give all the inscriptions for the place or family under consideration. Citations are arranged in three sequences, general, by place, and by family name.

A. GENERAL

GARDNER, ARTHUR. 'Alabaster tombs of the Gothic period,' *A.J.* **80**, 1923, 1-80. 14-15th c., includes list for the whole country.
KING, T.W. 'On the preservation of monumental inscriptions', *A.J.* **1**, 1845, 135-41. General discussion.
WALLER, J.G. 'Notes on the study of monumental brasses', *J.B.A.A.* **4**, 1849, 227-9.
WAY, ALBERT. 'Sepulchral brasses and incised slabs,' *A.J.* **1**, 1845, 197-212.
For wooden effigies, see below under Essex, Little Horkesley.

B. BY PLACE

Bedfordshire
ADDINGTON, H. 'The monumental brasses of Bedfordshire', *A.J.* **40**, 1883, 303-15.
ADDINGTON, H. 'The monumental brasses of Bedfordshire', *A.A.S.R.P.* **17**(1), 1883, 77-92.

Berkshire
OLIVER, ANDREW. 'Notes on the brasses of Berkshire', *JBAA*, N.S. **12**(1), 1906, 12-17.

Aldermaston
KEYSER, CHARLES E. 'Aldermaston Church, Berkshire', *A.J.* **55**, 1898, 367-96.

Buckinghamshire
Clifton Reynes
KELKE, W. HASTINGS. 'On three sepulchral monuments at Clifton Reynes in the county of Buckingham', *A.J.* **11**, 1854, 149-56.

Cheshire
WALLER, J.G. 'On certain church brasses in Cheshire and Lancashire', *J.B.A.A.* **5**, 1850, 256-65.

Cumberland
FERGUSON, R.S. 'The heraldry of the Cumberland statesmen', *A.J.* **48**, 1891, 77-82. Includes memorial inscriptions.

Derbyshire
KIRKE, HENRY. 'Derbyshire church notes', *Reliquary* **12**, 1871-2, 217-21. From the Dodsworth mss. at the Bodleian Library; includes many monumental inscriptions.
OLIVER, A. 'Notes on the incised effigies of Derbyshire and Staffordshire', *A.J.* **78**, 1921, 1-30. Includes list.
See also Devon. Plymouth.

Chapel en le Frith
KIRKE, HENRY. 'Church notes, Chapel-en-le-Frith', *Reliquary* **7**, 1866-7, 136-9. Includes monumental inscriptions and heraldry, with pedigree of Reynolds, 17-18th c.

Morley
GREAVES, C. 'Notes on brasses in Morley Church, near Derby', *A.J.* **33**, 1876, 290-3.

Staveley
SIMPSON, JUSTIN. 'Colonel Holles' church notes from Staveley, Derbyshire and Mansfield, Nottinghamshire', *Reliquary* **7**, 1866-7, 12-16. Heraldic notes etc.

Tideswell
'Epitaphs from Tideswell churchyard', *Reliquary* **6**, 1865-6, 246-8.

Whittington
CLARK, J.H. 'Church notes, Whittington, Derbyshire', *Reliquary* **6**, 1865-6, 199-200. Includes monumental inscriptions.

Devon

Branscombe
COX, J. CHARLES. 'The church of Branscombe', *Reliquary* N.S., **15**, 1909, 1-23. Includes some monumental inscriptions, with a list of vicars.

Plymouth
JEWITT, LLEWELLYN. 'Notes on some Derbyshire monuments in the churches of St Andrew and Charles, Plymouth', *Reliquary* **12**, 1871-2, 161-3.

Dorset

PRIDEAUX, W. DE C. 'The monumental brasses of Dorsetshire', *J.B.A.A.* N.S. 13, 1907, 210-26.

Co. Durham

Durham

HOWE, JOHN J. 'Monumental inscriptions in Durham Cathedral Yard', *N.G.* 1, 1895, 145-6.
'Monumental inscriptions in Durham Cathedral', *N.G.* 1, 1895, 55-6 & 107.

Essex

CHRISTY, MILLER, PORTEOUS, W.W., & SMITH, E. BERTRAM. 'Some interesting Essex brasses', *Reliquary* N.S. 5, 1899, 9-21; 7, 1901, 73-88; 9, 1903, 145-62; 14, 1908, 39-46 & 124-37.

Little Horkesley

MARKHAM, CLEMENTS ROBERT. 'Notes on Little Horkesley Church, Essex', *Arch.* 46, 1881, 269-80. Includes notes on monumental inscriptions, with list of wooden effigies throughout England.

Gloucestershire

DAVIS, CECIL T. 'The monumental brasses of Gloucestershire', *A.J.* 48, 1891, 19-28.
FRYER, A.C. 'Monumental effigies made by British craftsmen, 1240-1550', *Arch.* 74, 1925, 1-72. In Bristol, Gloucestershire, Wales, Somerset and various other counties.

Tewkesbury

LYSONS, SAMUEL. 'Observations on some of the tombs in the Abbey Church at Tewkesbury', *Arch.* 14, 1803, 143-53.

Hampshire

Brading

WHITEHEAD, DR. 'Notes on the church of St. Mary, Brading', *J.B.A.A.* N.S. 21 1915, 321-32. Includes notes on memorials.

Herefordshire

HAINES, HERBERT. 'The monumental brasses of the cathedral and county of Hereford', *J.B.A.A.* 27, 1871, 85-99, 198-203 & 541.

Much Marcle

BLOXHAM, M.H., & WALKER, J. SEVERN. 'Much Marcle church, Herefordshire: its architecture and monuments', *A.A.S.R.P.* 12(1), 1873, 145-52. Includes notes on monuments.

Hertfordshire

St. Albans

BOUTELL, CHARLES. 'The early heraldry of the Abbey Church of St. Alban, now St. Alban's Cathedral', *J.B.A.A.* 34, 1878, 16-30.

Huntingdonshire

Orton Longueville

ROYSTON, PETER. 'Orton Longueville Church', *J.B.A.A.* N.S. 5, 1899, 97-105. Includes 'copy of the epitaphs'.

Kent

Canterbury

GRIFFIN, R. 'Heraldry in the Chicheley porch of the cathedral church of Christ, Canterbury', *Arch.* 71, 1921, 125-32.
GRIFFIN, R. 'The heraldry in the cloisters of the cathedral church of Christ at Canterbury', *Arch.* 66, 1915, 447-568.

Otham

CAVE-BROWNE, J. 'Otham church and parish', *J.B.A.A.* N.S. 1, 1895, 167-86.

Lancashire

See Cheshire.

Leicestershire

BLOXAM, MATTHEW HOLBECHE. 'On some of the sephulchral monuments and effigies in Leicestershire', *A.A.S.R.P.* 8(2), 1866, 312-9.

Bottesforde

BLOXAM, MATTHEW HOLBECHE. 'On the sepulchral effigies in Bottesford church, Leicestershire', *A.A.S.R.P.* 10(1), 1869, 146-52.

Melton Mowbray

WING, VINCENT. 'An enquiry concerning the founders and ancient monuments of Melton Mowbray church', *A.A.S.R.P.* 8(1), 1865, 171-85.

Lincolnshire

SIMPSON, JUSTIN. 'Heraldry in Lincolnshire churches in the time of Charles the First, from Holle's mss in the British Museum', *Reliquary* **23**, 1882-3, 29-32, 76-80 & 141-4; **24**, 1883-4, 63.

SIMPSON, JUSTIN. 'Lincolnshire church notes of the time of Charles I', *Reliquary* **9**, 1868-9, 41-8. Includes a few monumental inscriptions from various churches.

Bardney

FOWLER, J.T. 'Tombstone inscriptions from Bardney Abbey', *A.A.S.R.P.* **32**(2), 1914, 403-10.

Boston

BLOXAM, M.H. 'Sepulchral monuments and effigies in Boston church, Lincolnshire', *A.A.S.R.P.* **10**(2), 1870, 219-23.

Lincoln

BLOXAM, MATTHEW HOLBECHE. 'On the tombs in Lincoln Cathedral'. *A.A.S.R.P.* **18**(2) 1886, 103-10.

LINCOLN, PRECENTOR. 'The memorial slabs formerly in the cloisters of Lincoln Minster', *A.A.S.R.P.* **21**(2), 1892, 190-4. Notes on 42 slabs.

Spilsby

TROLLOPE, EDWARD. 'St James's Church, Spilsby', *A.A.S.R.P.* **8**(1), 1865, 1-37. Mainly concerned with monuments of Willoughby and Bertie families.

Uffington

SIMPSON, JUSTIN. 'Some account of the village of Uffington, county of Lincoln, its church, and monuments therein, &c., &c', *Reliquary* **6**, 1865-6, 220-3, & **7**, 1866-7, 72-7. See also **7**, 1866-7, 126-7. Includes monumental inscriptions.

London and Middlesex

Fulham

WOODHOUSE, T.J. 'Notice of a newly compiled register of tombs in Fulham Church, etc', *J.B.A.A.* **43**, 1887, 328-34.

St. Helen, Bishopsgate

BARTON, R. HARVEY. 'The ancient church of St. Helen, Bishopsgate', *J.B.A.A.* N.S. 17, 1911, 97-108. Includes notes on memorials.

St. Olave, Hart Street

CORCORAN, BRYAN. 'The church of St. Olave, Hart Street', *J.B.A.A.* N.S. 17, 1911, 111-28. Includes notes on some memorials.

Norfolk

DRAKE, WILLIAM. 'Sepulchral brasses: notice of interesting memorials in Norfolk and other counties', *A.J.* **2**, 1847, 243-50. Includes list of Warwickshire brasses.

Hindolvestone

ANDRE, J. LEWIS. 'Hindolvestone church, Norfolk', *Reliquary* N.S. 7, 1893, 28-33. Includes monumental inscriptions.

Kings Lynn

CAMERON, H.K. 'The fourteenth century Flemish brasses at King's Lynn', *A.J.* **136**, 1979, 151-72.

Norwich

COMPTON, C.H. 'Notes on the church of St Michael Coslaney, Norwich', *J.B.A.A.* **42**, 1886, 395-9.

Northamptonshire

BLOXAM, MATTHEW HOLBECHE. 'On the medieval sepulchral antiquities of Northamptonshire', *A.J.* **35**, 1878, 242-62.

MARKHAM, CHRISTOPHER A. 'Hatchments', *A.A.S.R.P.* **30**(2), 1910, 673-759. Includes list of those in Northamptonshire churches.

Croughton

KEYSER, CHARLES E. 'A visit to the churches of Croughton, Northamptonshire and Hanwell, Horley and Hornton, Oxfordshire', *J.B.A.A.* **27**, 1921, 129-58. Includes some inscriptions.

Nottinghamshire

Flawford

LOWE, A.E. LAWSON. 'Flawford church, Nottinghamshire', *Reliquary* **15**, 1874-5, 1-6. Includes monumental inscriptions.

Mansfield

See Derbyshire. Staveley.

Tuxford

SIMPSON, JUSTIN. 'The notes of Gervase Holles on Tuxford church, and Haughton Hall, Notts', *Reliquary* **22**, 1881-2, 239-40. Heraldry.

Oxfordshire

Chickendon
See South Stoke

Hanwell, Horley, Hornton
See Northamptonshire, Croughton

Ipsden
See South Stoke

North Stoke
See South Stoke

Oxford
HOPE, W.H. ST. JOHN. 'Heraldry and sculptures of the vault of the Divinity School at Oxford', *A.J.* 71, 1914, 217-60. Includes list of arms.

South Stoke
KEYSER, CHARLES E. 'Notes on the churches of South Stoke, North Stoke, Ipsden, and Chickendon, Oxfordshire', *J.B.A.A.* N.S. 24, 1918, 1-32. Includes inscriptions.

Shropshire

STEPHENSON, MILL. 'Monumental brasses in Shropshire', *A.J.* 52, 1895, 47-103. Includes many genealogical notes.
MASTER, GEORGE STREYNSHAM. 'Sepulchral brasses: a collection of rubbings exhibited at Ludlow congress, 1867', *J.B.A.A.* 24, 1868, 382-7. Mainly from Shropshire and Wales.

Albrighton
PLANCHE, J.R. 'On an altar tomb at Albrighton, County Salop', *J.B.A.A.* 32, 1876, 32-43. Probably memorial of Andrew Fitz Nicholas de Willeley. Includes much genealogical information on Pichford family.

Wroxeter
SCARTH, H.M. 'The church and monuments of Wroxeter', *J.B.A.A.* 17, 1861, 85-99. Includes notes on Newport family, 14-17th c.

Somerset
See also Gloucestershire.

Bicknoller
MARSHALL, GEORGE W. 'Monumental inscriptions from Bicknoller, Co. Somerset', *Reliquary* 14, 1873-4, 235-6.

Staffordshire
See Derbyshire.

Surrey

Stoke D'Abernon
CLIFT, J.G.N. 'The Stoke D'Abernon brasses', *J.B.A.A.* N.S. 15 1909, 77-11.

Sussex

Chichester
BLOXAM, M.H. 'Sepulchral effigies at Chichester', *J.B.A.A.* 42, 1886, 287-93.

Wales
See Shropshire.

Warwickshire
See also Norfolk.

Warwick
HARTSHORNE, ALBERT. 'On the monuments and effigies in St. Mary's Church and the Beauchamp Chapel, Warwick', *A.J.* 45, 1888, 238-56.

Wixford
WADLEY, T.P. 'Wixford church, Warwickshire', *A.A.S.R.P.* 14(2), 1978, 304-8. Includes notes on monuments of Clopton, Griffin and Lingen families.

Wiltshire

Fonthill
SIMPSON, JUSTIN. 'An account of the armorial decorations formerly in the windows of Fonthill Abbey, Wilts', *Reliquary* 7, 1866-7, 109-12 & 167-72.

Salisbury
PLANCHE, J. R. 'On the sepulchral effigies in Salisbury Cathedral', *J.B.A.A.* 15, 1859, 115-30.

Worcestershire

Bredon
KEYSER, CHARLES E. 'An architectural account of Bredon Church, Worcestershire', *J.B.A.A.* N.S. 18, 1912, 1-12. Includes notes on memorials.

Yorkshire

Hull
WALTER, D. ALLEYNE. 'The armorial ledger stones in the church of the Holy Trinity,

Hull', *Reliquary* N.S. **2**, 1888, 129-32 & 215; **3**, 1889, 41-2, 89-90 & 168.

Sheffield
COLLIER, CARUS VALE. 'Notes on the heraldry in the parish church of Sheffield', *Reliquary* N.S. **4**, 1890, 212-8.

Woodkirk
MORKHILL, J.W. 'Inscriptions in the burial place at Tingley House, par. Woodkirk', *N.G.* **2**, 1896, 206-7. Includes will of John Pickering, 1699.

C. BY FAMILY

Ainslie
LAYARD, FLORENCE. 'An account of the metal plate and epitaph on St. Margaret's Tower in the old churchyard, Lee, Kent', *Reliquary* N.S. **4**, 1890, 224-8. Monumental inscription to Bryan Ainslie, with much genealogical information.

Aston
COCKAYNE, ANDREAS EDWARD. 'On the Aston monuments in St. Mary's Church, Stafford, embracing a very brief sketch of the Aston family', *J.B.A.A.* **29**, 1873, 294-301.

Atkins
GROVER, J. W. 'Discovery of the Atkins monument at Clapham', *J.B.A.A.* **42**, 1886, 272-8. Includes several inscriptions.

Ayscough
HAWKESBURY, LORD. 'The Ayscough monuments at Stallingborough, Co. Lincoln', *N.G.* **2**, 1896, 43-4.

Beauchamp
DILLON, VISCOUNT. 'The Warwick effigy', *A.J.* **73**, 1916, 207-11. Richard Beauchamp, 1439.

Bellingham
FISHER, J. 'The Bellingham tomb in Kendal church', *Reliquary* **4**, 1863-4, 63.

Beton
JEWITT, LLEWELLYN. 'Sepulchral brass to John Beton in Edensor church, Derbyshire', *Reliquary* **13**, 1872-3, 64-6. 1570.

Boynton
'Roxby and the brass of Thomas Boynton, esquire', *Reliquary* N.S. **7**, 1803, 97-100. Yorkshire, 1520.

Broham
BROUGHAM, WILLIAM. 'The tombs of the De Broham family, with an account of some remarkable discoveries recently made in their burial-place in the church of Brougham', *A.J.* **4**, 1847, 59-68.

Catesby
SERJEANTSON, R.M. 'The restoration of the long-lost brass of Sir Wm. Catesby', *A.A.S.R.P.* **31**(2), 519-24. Northamptonshire; 1472.

Chandos
MEYRICK, SAMUEL RUSH. 'Account of the tomb of Sir John Chandos, Knt., A.D. 1370, at Civaux, a hamlet on the Vienne in France', *Arch.* **20**, 1824, 484-95. Herefordshire and Monmouthshire; includes pedigree, 13-14th c.

Cheyne
KELKE, W. HASTINGS. 'An account of two monumental effigies found at Chenies, Buckinghamshire', *A.J.* **10**, 1853, 44-52. Cheyne family, c.1400.

Clare
WALFORD, WESTON S. 'On an inscribed stone coffin-lid in the ancient cemetery of the Temple Church, London', *A.J.* **20**, 1863, 138-40. Memorial of Roger de Clare, Earl of Hertford, 1173.

Cokayne
PLANCHE, J.R. 'Monuments of the Cokayne family in Ashbourne Church, Derbyshire', *J.B.A.A.* **7**, 1851, 374-83. Medieval.

Coulthirst
'Monumental brass of Robert Coulthirst at Kirkleatham', *Reliquary* N.S. **6**, 1892, 49-50. Yorkshire; 1631.

Courtenay
ROGERS, WILLIAM HENRY HAMILTON. 'Some account of the Courtenay tomb in Colyton Church, Devon', *Arch.* **48**, 1885, 157-66.
WYATT, H. S. 'Monuments in the parish

church, Colyton, Devon', *J.B.A.A.* N.S. **33**,
1927, 140-44. Courtenay, Pole and Westover
monuments.

Cranford
CLIFT, J.G.N. 'Brass of Edward Cranford',
J.B.A.A. N.S. **14**, 1908, 263-5. Puttenham,
Surrey, 1431.

Culpeper
See Haitfield.

De Burgh
MANNING, C. R. 'Monuments of the De
Burgh and Ingoldsthorpe families in Burgh
Green Church, Cambridgeshire', *A.J.* **34**,
1877, 121-9. Includes pedigrees of De Burgh
of Burgh Green, and of Ingoldsthorpe of
Rainham, Norfolk; medieval.

De La Beche
WALFORD, WESTON S. 'Effigy in Aldworth
Church, Berks., with some notice of the De
La Beche family of that county', *A.J.* **14**,
1857, 144-59. 13-14th c. monument, probably
of De La Beche family.

De La Pole
MANNING, C.J. 'Notice of an undescribed
sepulchral brass', *A.J.* **4**, 1847, 338-40. At
Saffron Walden, Essex; memorial of John
and Joan De La Pole, 15th c. Includes
pedigree.

Dykes
See Wenslygh.

Echyngham
HALL, SPENCER. 'Notices of sepulchral
memorials at Etchingham, Sussex, and of the
church at that place', *A.J.* **7**, 1850, 265-73.
14th c. memorials of Echyngham family.

Fettiplace
PLANCHE, J.R. 'On the monument of a
supposed princess of Portugal in East
Shefford Church, Berkshire', *J.B.A.A.* **16**,
1860, 145-57. Beatrice Fettiplace, 1447.
Includes genealogical notes.

Fitzralph
PIGGOT, JOHN. 'Notes on the brass of Sir
William Fitz-Ralph, c.1323, in Pebmarsh
church, Essex', *Reliquary* **9**, 1868-9, 193-200.

Fitzherbert
See Montgomery.

Fleming
CAMERON, H.K. 'Flemish brasses to civilians
in England', *A.J.* **139**, 1982, 420-40. Brasses
of Alan Fleming, Newark, Nottinghamshire,
1361; Thomas de Topclyff, Yorkshire, 1362;
Roger Thornton, Newcastle-on-Tyne, 1429.

Foix
PLANCHE, J. R. 'Obervations on an effigy
called that of William de Foix, in
Winchester Cathedral', *J.B.A.A.* **1**, 1846, 216-
23. 14th c?

Foljambe
FOLJAMBE, CECIL G. SAVILE. 'Monumenta
Foljambeana: the Foljambe chapel in the
south aisle of the choir of Chesterfield
church', *Reliquary* **14**, 1873-4, 65-70 & 237-
42; **15**, 1874-5, 25-33. Includes monumental
inscriptions, parish register extracts, and
medieval pedigree.

Fynderne
JEWITT, LL. 'Brass of William Fynderne of
Childney, Berkshire', *Reliquary* **4**, 1863-4,
62-3.

Gaveston
W., W.S. 'Remarks on an effigy of a knight
in Winchester Cathedral', *A.J.* **15**, 1858, 125-
36. Probably of Sir Arnold de Gaveston; includes genealogical notes.

Giffarde
See Montgomery.

Gifford
PLANCHE, J.R. 'On the effigy of a lady in
Worcester Cathedral', *J.B.A.A.* **6**, 1851, 5-15.
Probably Margaret Gifford, 14th c.

Grey
EGERTON, SIR PHILIP GREY. 'On a
monumental brass in Christ's Church
Cathedral, Dublin', *A.J.* **36**, 1879, 213-8. Grey
family at Wilton, Wiltshire, 16-17th c.
KING, THOMAS WILLIAM. 'Observations on
the monumental inscription to Richard Grey,
Lord Grey de Wilton, in the chapel of Eton
College, Bucks', *Arch.* **32**, 1847, 58-9. Wilton,
Wiltshire, 1521; includes pedigree, 14-16th c.

Haitfield

DAVIES, RANDALL. 'On some brasses illustrating civilian and female dress', *Reliquary* N.S., 1, 1887, 109-11. Robert de Haitfield, Owston, Yorkshire, 1417; John Urban, Southfleet, Kent, 1420; Elizabeth Culpeper, West Peckham, Kent, c.1469; Anne Thompson, Bearden, Essex, 1607.

MANNING, C. R. 'Notes on a brass of Robert de Haitfield and Ada, his wife, Owston Church, Yorkshire', *A.J.* 36, 1879, 172-3. 1417.

Harrington

'The monumental brass and will of Christopher Harrington, goldsmith, of York, 1614', *Reliquary* N.S. 6, 1892, 211-5. Also includes will of Thomas Harrington, 1642.

Hastings

HARTSHORNE, A. 'On the brass of Sir Hugh Hastings in Elsing Church, Norfolk', *Arch.* 60, 1906, 25-42.

Hatfeild

See Wilmot.

Hervey

BLOXAM, MATTHEW HOLBECHE. 'On the incised brass effigy in Elstow church of Elizabeth Hervey, Abbess of Elstow', *A.A.S.R.P.* 7(1), 1863, 127-31. Bedfordshire; 16th c.

Hillary

HEWITT, JOHN. 'Monumental effigy of Sir Roger de Hillary', *A.J.* 31, 1874, 153-6. Walsall, Staffordshire; 14th c.

Hoare

HOARE, EDWARD. 'On the memorial sepulchral brass in Hayes Church, near Bromley, Kent, over the grave of the Rev. John Hoare, rector of that parish', *A.J.* 28, 1881, 229-31. 1584.

Howard

STONE, LAWRENCE, & COLVIN, HOWARD. 'The Howard tomb at Framlingham, Suffolk', *A.J.* 122, 1965, 159-71.

MARKS, RICHARD. 'The Howard tombs at Thetford and Framlingham: new discoveries', *A.J.* 141, 1984, 252-68. Suffolk; includes pedigree, 15-16th c.

Ingoldsthorpe

See De Burgh.

Langley

EVANS, JOAN. 'Edmund of Langley and his tomb', *Arch.* 46, 1881, 297-325. Son of Edward III. Tomb at Kings Langley, Hertfordshire.

Liddell

DAVIS, CECIL T. 'Monumental brass in the Old or West Church, Aberdeen', *A.J.* 51, 1894, 76-80. To Dr. Duncan Liddell, 1613.

Lisle

WALLER, J. G. 'On the brass of Sir John de Lisle', *J.B.A.A.* 3, 1848, 240-2. At Thruxton, Hampshire, 1407.

Longespee

CARRINGTON, F. A. 'On monumental figures discovered at Wanborough, Wilts', *J.B.A.A.* 7, 1852, 52-6. Probably of the Longespee family; medieval.

Lowther

JEWITT, LL. 'Curious monumental pedigree inscription, Lowther church, Westmoreland', *Reliquary* 17, 1876-7, 191-2. Lowther family pedigree on monumental inscription, 1607.

Lyfelde

RICE, R.G. 'Lyfelde monument at Stoke D'Abernon', *Reliquary* 13, 1872-3, 255-6. Surrey; monumental inscription, 1592, with pedigree.

Markenfield

PLANCHE, J. R. 'On an effigy of one of the Markenfield family in Ripon Cathedral, *J.B.A.A.* 20, 1864, 285-96. Yorkshire; Sir Thomas Markenfield, 14th c. Includes genealogical notes.

Mauley

MEYRICK, SIR SAMUEL. 'Observations on the monumental effigy of De Mauley, formerly in the Minster of York', *Arch.* 1846, 238-48. Includes medieval pedigree.

Montfort

HARTSHORNE, ALBERT. 'Notes on an effigy attributed to Richard Wellesborne de Montfort, and other sepulchral memorials in

Hughenden Church, Buckinghamshire, *A.J.* 34, 1877, 279-90. 14-15th c., Montfort family.

Montgomery
JEWITT, LLEWELLYN. 'A note on some armorial bearings on the tower of Cubley church, Derbyshire', *Reliquary* 15, 1874-5, 7-8. Includes pedigree of Montgomery of Cubley, and its alliances with Fitzherbert, Giffarde, et al; medieval.

Moore
MITCHINSON, BISHOP. 'The brass of John Moore, M.A., 1532, at Sibstone, Leicestershire', *Reliquary* N.S. 7, 1893, 193-4.

Palaeologus
JAGO, VIVYAN. 'Some observations on a monumental inscription in the parish church of Landulph, Cornwall', *Arch.* 18, 1817, 83-104. Monumental inscription to Theodore Palaeologus, 1636; includes pedigrees of Palaeologus, Lower, Arundel and Killigrew.

Pole
See Courtenay.

Rothwell
SERJEANTSON, R.M. 'William de Rothwell and his brass', *A.A.S.R.P.* 30(2), 1910, 665-72. Northamptonshire; 14th c.

St. Leger
ROBERTSON, W.A. SCOTT. 'Discovery of an unrecorded monumental brass', *Reliquary* N.S. 8, 1894, 233-5. Commemorating Thomas St. Leger, 1408.

Salwey
BLOXAM, M.H. 'Monument in Stanford church, Worcestershire', *A.A.S.R.P.* 10(2), 1870, 306-7. To Humphrey Salwey, 1444.

Sandys
BLOXAM, MATTHEW HOLBECHE. 'On the sepulchral effigy of Archbishop Sandys, in the minster church, Southwell, Nottinghamshire', *A.A.S.R.P.* 10(1), 1869, 27-38.

Selley
WALTER, D. ALLEYNE. 'Monumental slab, Gorhill church, East Yorks', *Reliquary* N.S. 3, 1889, 193-4. Monumental inscription to Joan Selley, c.15th c.

Seymour
BRAILSFORD, W. 'The monuments of the Seymours in Great Bedwyn Church, Wilts', *A.J.* 39, 1882, 407-9.

Sothill
THORPE, MISS. 'The Sothill tomb in Redbourne church, near Kirton-in-Lindsey, Lincolnshire', *Reliquary* 15, 1874-5, 154. Medieval.

Stanley
HEWITT, J. 'Stanley monument in Lichfield Cathedral', *A.J.* 24, 1867, 222-5. See also 226-8. Includes genealogical notes.

Sulney
HEWITT, J. 'Effigies of the De Sulneys at Newton Solney, Derbyshire', *A.J.* 7, 1850, 360-9. Medieval; includes genealogical notes.

Talbot
STACYE, JOHN. 'On the monuments in the Shrewsbury Chapel in parish church, Sheffield', *J.B.A.A.* 30, 1874, 175-81. Talbot family memorials.

Thompson
See Haitfield.

Thornton
See Fleming.

Topclyffe
See Fleming.

Trumpington
SPITTLE, S. D. T. 'The Trumpington brass', *A.J.* 127, 1970, 223-7. Cambridgeshire; includes pedigree of Trumpington, 13-14th c.

Turner
'The brass of Dorothy Turner at Kirkleatham', *Reliquary* N.S. 8, 1894, 116-8. Yorkshire; 1628.

Urban
See Haitfield.

Warre
BURGES, W. 'The tomb and helm of Thomas La Warre in the church at Broadwater, Sussex', *A.J.* 36, 1879, 78-87. 1526.

Wenslygh

RAINE, JAMES, 'Notes of a remarkable sepulchral brass of Flemish design, in the church of Wensley, Yorkshire', *A.J.* **12**, 1855, 238-43. Memorials to Simon de Wenslygh, 14th c., and Oswald Dykes, 1607.

Westover

See Courtenay.

Willoughby

NOTTINGHAM, BISHOP OF. 'Grimsthorpe and the Willoughby monuments in Edenham church', *A.A.S.R.P.* **20**(1) 1889, 19-24. Includes genealogical notes on Willoughby family.

Wilmot

'Wilmot and Hatfeild families: monumental inscription in Duffield church', *Reliquary* **22**, 1881-2, 127. 17-18th c.

3. ROLLS OF ARMS ETC

General articles on heraldry which are not of direct genealogical interest have been excluded from this bibliography. However, rolls of arms and other listings of arms may be of value, and are noted below. Heraldic inscriptions are dealt with in section 2.

FLETCHER, W.G.D. 'Arms of Derbyshire knights, temp Edward I', *Reliquary* **22**, 1881-2, 64.
FLETCHER, W.G.DIMOCK. 'Heraldic grants to Derbyshire families', *Reliquary* **22**, 1881-2, 49-52, 240 & 244-5. 16-17th c.
FOLBY, F. T. 'The heraldry of Exeter', *A.J.* **30**, 1873, 235-63. Private arms on public display in the city; includes index.
GREENSTREET, JAMES, & RUSSELL, CHARLES. 'The Dering roll of arms', *Reliquary* **16**, 1875-6, 135-40 & 237-40; **17**, 1876-7, 11-16 & 209-12; **18**, 1877-8, 23-8, 89-92 & 171-5.
GREENSTREET, JAMES. 'The Falkirk roll of arms', *Reliquary* **16**, 1875-6, 27-32 & 68-74.
GREENSTREET, JAMES. 'Jenyns roll of arms as an ordinary', *Reliquary* **26**, 1885-6, 33-40, 97-104 & 129-36. Includes index.

GREENSTREET, JAMES. 'The Nativity roll of arms, temp. Edward I', *Reliquary* **15**, 1874-5, 228-30.
GREENSTREET, JAMES. 'The original Camden roll of arms', *J.B.A.A.* **38**, 1882, 309-28. Includes genealogical notes.
GREENSTREET, JAMES. 'The Powell roll of arms (temp Edward III)', *Reliquary* N.S. **3**, 1889, 145-52 & 231-40; **4**, 1890, 93-7.
KING, T.W. 'Collection of mss. in Coll. Arm, for Co. Suffolk', *J.B.A.A.* **21**, 1865, 158-9.
LOWE, A.E. LAWSON. 'A Nottinghamshire armory', *Reliquary* **15**, 1874-5, 231-4; **16**, 1875-6, 49-52, 107-11, 159-62 & 229-32; **19**, 1878-9, 29-32 & 201-4; **20**, 1879-80, 49.
PERCEVAL, CHARLES SPENCER. 'Two rolls of arms of the reign of King Edward the first', *Arch.* **39**(2), 1864, 389-446.
SLEIGH, JOHN. 'A Derbyshire armory', *Reliquary* **5**, 1864-5, 227-34; **6**, 1865-6, 38-44.
SLEIGH, JOHN. 'A Derbyshire armory: addenda and corrigenda', *Reliquary,* **12**, 1871-2, 93-6.
STEPHENSON, MILL & GRIFFIN, RALPH. 'A roll of arms belonging to the Society, temp. Henry VIII, c.1540', *Arch.* **69**, 1918, 61-110.
WALFORD, W. S. 'Notice of a roll of arms belonging to Wilkinson Mathews, esq., Q.C.', *A.J.* **17**, 1860, 218-23.
WALFORD, WESTON STYLEMAN. 'A roll of arms of the thirteenth century', *Arch.* **39**(2) 1864, 373-88.

4. PROBATE RECORDS

A. GENERAL

'Act books of the Perogative Court of Canterbury', *N.G.* **2**, 1896, 13-16, 63-6 & 187-90; **3**, 1900, 44-7, 75-8, 116-23 & 173-6; **4**, 1901, 19-21 & 85-8. Brief abstracts, 1679-89, relating to northern counties.
'Four goldsmiths' wills', *Reliquary* N.S. **7**, 1893, 111-13. Includes wills of John Haster of Kirkham, 1511; Thomas Wardell of Hull, 1531; William Whithalce of Doncaster, 1534; and Edmund Kendall of Gisburne, 1547.
'Modern depositories of ancient wills', *N.G.* **1**, 1895, 219-21. List, now superseded.
'Naval and military notes', *N.G.* **1**, 1895, 248-50. Wills of Zacharias Laurentious, 1795;

John Dawson of York, 1747; Isaac Green, 1740; Thomas Hilary, 1744; John Lind of Hull, 1775 and Wm. Moorfoot of Lund, 1783, with obituary notes on Mary King, 1831, L. Lacey 1819; Chas. Mason, 1812 and ? Nelson, 1808.
'Some physicians' wills', *N.G.* **2**, 1896, 87-8. Wills of Christ. Milner of York, 1607, William Ward of Whitby, 1768; Ralph Bourchier of St. George the Martyr, Middlesex, 1767 and Henry Iveson of Norwich, 1766.

B. BY PLACE

Cheshire
See Lancashire.

Cumberland
'Cumberland and Westmoreland wills', *N.G.* **1**, 1895, 174-6. Wills of John Hudson of Bowtherbecke, 1609; Sir Edward Musgrave of Hatton Castle, 1673; both Cumberland; Christopher Middleton of Deansbiginge, c. 1603; James Bellingham of Over Levens, 1678; both Westmorland.
'Cumberland and Westmoreland wills', *N.G.* **1**, 1895, 234-9. Wills of Deborah Baynes of Appleby, 1729; Sir Wm. Fleming of Rydall, 1734; both Westmorland, James Adderton of Penrith, Cumberland, 1726.
'Cumberland wills', *N.G.* **3**, 1900, 144-5. Wills of Henry Fletcher Partis, 1775, John Langton, 1776, Mary Grayburne, 1794, John Dodgson, 1778, and Thomas Irwen, 1778.

Derbyshire
'Derbyshire and Leicestershire wills', *N.G.* **1**, 1895, 147-51. Wills of Thomas Hulley of Ashover, 1587; Arthur Turner of Parkhouse, 1706; German Pole of Radburne, 1702; Ann Pole of Radburne, 1703; all Derbyshire; John Hawford of Keyworth, 1603; Henry Watters of Belvoir Castle, 1729; both Leicestershire.

Co. Durham
ORNSBY, GEORGE. 'On Durham wills and inventories', *J.B.A.A.* **22**, 1866, 396-420. General discussion of their contents.

Kent
DUNKIN, E.H.W. 'Testamentary notices of churches in West Kent', *Reliquary* **18**, 1877-8, 203-5. Bequests to churches, 1440-1573.

Lancashire
WILKINSON, T.T. 'Manchester wills and inventories during the sixteenth century', *Reliquary* **14**, 1873-4, 221-4; **15**, 1874-5, 21-4. Brief extracts from many wills.
'Lancashire and Cheshire wills', *N.G.* **1**, 1895, 228-33. Wills of Francis Fitton of Gawsworth, 1608; Thomas Malbon of Congleton, 1775; both Cheshire; Thomas Massey of Liverpool, 1773; Betty Hawcourt of Manchester, 1775; Tyzack Trotter of Liverpool, 1778; all Lancashire.
'Lancashire wills', *N.G.* **1**, 1895, 177-9. Wills of Isabel Gooddaie, 1602; Richard Wade, 1610; George Smyth, 1609; James Ridehalgh, 1673; Richard Atherton, 1724 and Thomas Sprowell, 1730.

Leicestershire
See Derbyshire.

Lincolnshire
FOSTER, C.W. 'Lincolnshire wills proved in the Prerogative Court of Canterbury', *A.A.S.R.P.* **41**(1), 1934, 61-116; **41**(2), 1935, 179-218. 1384-1490.
MADDISON, A.R. 'Domestic life in the sixteenth and seventeenth centuries, illustrated by wills in the Registry at Lincoln', *A.A.S.R.P.* **17**(1) 1883, 21-30.
SMITH, W.H. 'An analytical calendar of Lincoln wills proved in the Prerogative Court of Canterbury', *N.G.* **1**, 1895, 211-5; **2**, 1896, 23-6, 59-62, 131-4 & 195-7; **3**, 1900, 132-7; **4**, 1901, 22-7; **5**, 1902, 109-15; **6**, 1903, 23-30. 16th c.
'Wills and administrations in the Peculiar Courts at Lincoln', *N.G.* **1**, 1895, 42-5, 80-87 & 162-4; **2**, 1896, 172-5. Caister prebendal court, 1636-1833; and Louth prebendal court, 1659-1837.

Northamptonshire
COX, J.C. 'The parish churches of Northamptonshire, illustrated by wills, temp. Henry VIII', *A.J.* **58**, 1901, 113-32.
SERJEANTSON, R. M. & LONGDEN, H.I. 'The parish churches and religious houses of Northamptonshire; their dedications, altars, images and lights', *A.J.* **70**, 1913, 217-432. Alphabetical list by parish, giving names of benefactors and extracts from their wills, 1510-58.

Nottinghamshire

'Manor court of Edwinstowe, Co. Notts: wills, administrations and inventories', *N.G.* 1, 1895, 20-24. List.

Westmorland

'Westmoreland wills', *N.G.* 2, 1896, 34-6. Wills of John Bracken, 1753; Robert Lowther, 1731; John Robinson, 1743-4 and Miles North, 1784.
See also Cumberland.

Worcestershire

ADAMS, G.F. 'Some old wills', *A.A.S.R.P.* 32(2), 1914, 502-14. Includes extracts from wills of Edmund Gower of Alcester, 1617; John Gower of Stone, 1609; Thomas Warmstry, Dean of Worcester, 1665; William Warmstry of Worcester, 1581; John Wall, 1589; Agnes Philps of Priors Cleve, 1557; Maud Ordymer, 1494; Phillip Ballard als Harvard of Elmley Lovett, 1557.

Yorkshire

BOYLE, J.B. 'Wills enrolled in the Liber Rubeus of Kingston-upon-Hull', *N.G.* 2, 1896, 181-3.
COOK, R. BEILBY. 'Some early civic wills of York', *A.A.S.R.P.* 28(2), 1906, 827-71; 31(1), 1911, 319-39; 32(1), 1913, 293-317; 32(2), 1914, 569-93; 33(1), 1915, 161-77; 33(2), 1916, 473-92; 34(1), 1917, 201-17; 35(1), 61-74. Medieval wills.
RAINE, CANON. 'On some early monuments of Conisborough', *A.A.S.R.P.* 9(1) 1867, 69-74. Mainly extracts from wills.
'Aldbrough manor court (West Riding)', *N.G.* 4, 1901, 65. List of wills, 17th c.
'Manor court of Altofts in Normanton, Co. York: wills and administration', *N.G.* 1, 1895, 130.
'Manor court of Arkengarthdale: original wills', *N.G.* 4, 1901, 93-102 & 116-31; 5, 1902, 24-29; 6, 1903, 93-6. Incomplete, reached 'Milner' when *N.G.* ceased publication.
'Manor court of Warmfield with Heath, Co. York: wills and administration', *N.G.* 1, 1895, 129. List.
'Peculiar court of Masham: a collation of the indexes at Somerset House and at York Probate Registry from the commencement down to 1709', *N.G.* 4, 1901, 132-6; 5, 1902, 30-32, 103-5 & 153-6; 6, 1903, 16-22 & 86-89. Incomplete; alphabetical arrangement to Rownthwaite only.

'Richmondshire wills (Eastern deaneries), being a calendar to the probate records formerly in the custody of the Archdeacon of Richmond', *N.G.* 2, 1896, supplement. Incomplete; to Gristhwaite only.
'Some wills from the Richmond registry', *N.G.* 3, 1900, 25-8, 109-12 & 124-30; 4, 1901, 41-8. Many abstracts.
'Wills &c., in the peculiar courts at Wakefield', *N.G.* 1, 1895, 33-7 & 110-12; 2, 1896, 102-7 & 168-71. 17-19th c.

C. ROYALTY

James II

FERRERS, EDMUND '... an authenticated copy of the will of King James the Second, with an inventory of the goods and chattels belonging to that monarch at the time of his death', *Arch.* 18, 1917, 223-39.

John

BIRCH, WALTER DE GRAY. 'Notes on the will of King John', *J.B.A.A.* 43, 1887, 335-9.

D. BY FAMILY

Achonry, Bishop of

GUNNER, W. H. 'Original document', *A.J.* 9, 1852, 358-60. Includes will of Simon, Bishop of Achonry, 1397, an Irish bishop probably employed as a suffragan in Hampshire.

Alleyne

FLETCHER, W.G. DIMOCK. 'Further notes on the Alleyne family of Co. Derby', *Reliquary* 23, 1882-3, 208. Wills and inquisitions post mortem, 16-18th c.

Almack

'Original documents', *A.J.* 5, 1848, 316-21. Includes wills of John and Richard Almack of Sandhutton, Yorkshire, 1558.

Ashe

'Original documents', *Reliquary* 8, 1867-8, 59-60. Will of John Ashe of Ashford-in-the-Water, Derbyshire, 1733.

Bagshaw

RICE, R.G. 'Abstract of the will of Nicholas Bagshawe of Wilkinhill, Co. Derby, 1656', *Reliquary* 19, 1878-9, 64.
'Original document', *Reliquary* 6, 1865-6, 109. Probate inventory of Catharine Bagshaw of Milnehousedale, Derbyshire, 1695.

Bean

'Bean of Jamaica', *N.G.* 1, 1895, 131-2. Will of James Bean of Jamaica and Aldbrough, Yorkshire, 1766.

Bennett

RICE, ROBERT GARRAWAY. 'The will of Anthony Bennett of Chertsey, Co. Surrey, goldsmith', *Reliquary* 23, 1882-3, 20-67. 1656 (proved 1658-9).

Bindlose

'Lancashire wills', *N.G.* 2, 1896, 39-40. Will of Sir Robert Bindlose, 1629.

Bingham

BINGHAM, C. W. 'Inventory of the household and personal effects, farm-stock, &c, of Robert Bingham of Bingham's Melcombe, Dorset, dated 4th Elisabeth, A.D. 1561', *A.J.* 17, 1860, 151-7.

Bohun

TURNER, T. H. 'The will of Humprey de Bohun, Earl of Hereford and Essex, with extracts from the inventory of his effects, 1319-1322', *A.J.* 2, 1847, 339-49.

Bradshaw

'Inventory of the goods of Mr. Francis Bradshaw, 1653', *Reliquary* N.S. 4, 1890, 98-102. Bradshaw Hall, Chapel-en-leFrith, Derbyshire.
'The will of Henry Bradshaw, of Bradshaw, Co. Derby', *Reliquary* N.S. 4, 1890, 106-8. 1521.

Braybroke

BRAYBROKE, E. W. 'Original documents: will of Nicholas Braybroke, Canon of Exeter, A.D., 1399-1400', *A.J.* 31, 1874, 181-5.

Burton

'Will of Edward Burton of Long Eaton, Derbyshire, 1638', *Reliquary* N.S. 8, 1894, 220-3.

Butler

ASTLE, THOMAS. 'Extract from the will of Thomas, Earl of Ormond, dated 31 July 1515, from the register called Holder in the Prerogative office', *Arch.* 3, 1775, 20-1. Butler family.

Collyns

'The will and inventory of Richard Collyns, citizen and haberdasher of London, 1523', *Reliquary* N.S. 7, 1893, 104-9.

Cooper

'Sir Edmund Cooper, royalist and mayor of York', *N.G.* 1, 1896, 65-6. Includes will, 1670, and monumental inscription.

Courtenay

OLIVER, GEORGE. 'The will of Katherine, Countess of Devon, daughter of Edward IV, dated 2 May 1527', *A.J.* 10, 1853, 53-8. Courtenay family.

Cowton

'The will of John Cowton of Scarborough, goldsmith, 1558', *Reliquary* N.S. 8, 1894, 178-9.

Crusoe

See Selkirk.

Curwen

See Kellett.

Cuthbert

'William Cuthbert, esq., recorder of Newcastle', *N.G.* 2, 1896, 57-8. Northumberland; will, 1746.

Dene

DEANE, JOHN BATHURST. 'The will of Henry Dene, Archbishop of Canterbury, deceased 15 February 1502-3', *A.J.* 18, 1861, 256-67. Probably of Gloucestershire.

Donne

MOORE, A. PERCIVAL. 'Notes on the will of a medieval archdeacon', *A.A.S.R.P.* 27(2), 1904, 503-24. William Donne, archdeacon of Leicester, fl. 1354-85.

Doune

THOMPSON, A. HAMILTON. 'The will of Master William Doune, Archdeacon of Leicester, *A.J.* 72, 1915, 233-84. 1361.

Dunstall

REDFERN, FRANCIS. 'A brief notice of Captain Dunstall, of Exeter', *Reliquary* 6, 1865-6, 76-8. Includes genealogical notes and will, 1751. Also of Uxbridge, Middlesex.

Elmham
BURTT, JOSEPH. 'Will of Richard de Elmham, canon of the church of St. Martin le Grand, London, dated 26 June 1228', *A.J.* **24**, 1867, 340-44.

Eyre
'Copy of the will of Edward Eyre, of Hope', *Reliquary* **8**, 1867-8, 60-61.
'Original document', *Reliquary* **4**, 1863-4, 45-8. Will of Thomas Eyre of Rowtor, Derbyshire, 1717.

Fairfax
'Fairfax wills at Carlisle', *N.G.* **1**, 1895, 92-3. 1640-65.
'Fairfax wills at Worcester', *N.G.* **1**, 895, 94-5. 18-19th c.
'Fairfax wills of Norfolk and Suffolk', *N.G.* **1**, 1895, 49-53. Includes extracts from parish registers and marriage licences.

Fermor
SHIRLEY, EVELYN PHILIP. 'Extracts from the Fermor accounts, A.D. 1580', *A.J.* **8**, 1851, 179-86. Extract from the will of Thomas Fermor, of Somerton, Oxfordshire, with the accounts of his executor.

Fitzherbert
FITZHERBERT, REGINALD H.C. 'The will of the celebrated judge, Sir Anthony Fitzherbert', *Reliquary* **21**, 1880-81, 234-6. Norbury, Derbyshire, 1538.

Foxle
GUNNER, WILLIAM H. 'The will of Sir John de Foxle, of Apuldrefield, Kent, dated 5 November 1378', *A.J.* **15**, 1857, 267-77.

Franke
See Hempstone

Fromond
GUNNER, W. H. 'The will of John Fromond, benefactor to Winchester College' *A.J.* **16**, 1859, 166-73. Sparsholt, Hampshire, 1420.

Gargrave
'Gargrave of Nostell', *N.G.* **1**, 1895, 137-8. Will of Sir Cottom Gargrave, 1585.

Greene
'Nuncupative will of William Greene of Newark, plumber, 1641', *Reliquary* N.S. **8**, 1894, 223.

Grimston
HOWARD, JOSEPH JACKSON & PERCEVAL, CHARLES SPENCER, 'An holograph will of Edward Grimston, esquire, made in 1449', *Arch.* **45**(1) 1877, 124-6.

Hall
'Will of Robert Hall of Matlock, Derbyshire, 1622', *Reliquary* N.S. **8**, 1894, 219.

Hanmer
'Hanmer of Flintshire', *N.G.* **1**, 1895, 161. Will of Wenefride Hanmer, of Radford, Nottinghamshire, 1604. Flintshire family.

Harrison
SIMPSON, JUSTIN. 'Harrison of Sedbergh and Stamford', *N.G.* **1**, 1895, 165-6. Will of Reginald Harrison, 1594.

Hempstone
W., W. S. 'Testamentary documents relating to property at Totnes, Devon', *A.J.* **8**, 1851, 307-12. Wills of John Hempstone, 1393, and Ambrose Franke, 1483, both of Totnes.

Holbein
BLACK, WILLIAM HENRY. 'Discovery of the will of Hans Holbein', *Arch.* **39**(1), 1853, 1-18. London; 1543.

Holden
See Maior

Holles
WOOD, A.C. 'The family of Gervase Holles', *A.A.S.R.P.* **40**, 1930, 257-70. Lincolnshire; includes wills of Gervase Holles, 1625; Frescheville Holles, 1630; John Kington, 1617.

Howard
SHIRLEY, EVELYN PHILIP. 'An inventory of the effects of Henry Howard, K. G., Earl of Northampton, taken in 1614, with a transcript of his will', *Arch.* **42**(2), 1870, 347-78.

Kellett
ESHELBY, H.D. 'Some early Richmond wills', *N.G.* **6**, 1903, 1-2. William Kellett, of Whittingham, Northumberland, 15th c., John Curwen of Workington, Cumberland, 1530.

King
See Maior

Kington
See Holles.

Kyrke
'Original document', *Reliquary* 5, 1864-5, 173-4. Probate inventory of Henry Kyrke, of Chapel-en-le-Frith, Derbyshire, 1735.

Labbe
T., T. H. '[Inventory of Reginald Labbe, 1393]', *A.J.* 3, 1846, 65-6.

Langford
HOPPER, CLARENCE. 'Extracts from the will of a Ludlow tradesman' *J.B.A.A.* 24, 1868, 269-70. Actually extracts from the probate inventory of William Langford of Ludlow, 1553/4.

Lawe
'The will of Richard Lawe of Halifax, goldsmith, 1565', *Reliquary* N.S. 8, 1894, 179. Yorkshire.

Lee
'Original documents', *Reliquary* 2, 1861-2, 161-2. Probate inventory of George Lee of Sheffield, Yorkshire, 1649.
'[Probate inventory of Roger Lee of Sheffield, 1614]', *Reliquary* 2, 1861-2, 231-2.

Lowe
HOPE, W.H. ST. JOHN. 'The will of John Lowe, S.T.P., Bishop of Rochester', *Reliquary* N.S. 8, 1894, 34-6. 1433.

Maior
STEER, FRANCIS W. 'Smaller houses and their furnishings in the seventeenth and eighteenth centuries', *J.B.A.A.* 3rd series 21, 1958, 140-59. Includes probate inventories of Matthew Maior, of Stoughton, Sussex, 1657, John King of Shipley, Sussex, 1709, and Robert Holden of Steyning, Sussex, 1709.

Mallorie
'An ancient Richmond will (Sir William Mallorie, Knt., 1411)', *N.G.* 2, 1896, 48.

Marshall
MARSHALL, GEORGE W. 'Marshall administrations in P.C.C.', *Reliquary* 21,

1880-81, 39-50, 101-6, 179-81 & 245-50; 22, 1881-2, 25-32, 102-7 & 217-22. Includes pedigrees.

Montagu
SHIRLEY, EVELYN PHILIP. 'The will, inventory and funeral expenses of James Montagu, Bishop of Winchester, anno 1618', *Arch.* 44, 1871, 393-421.

Morton
THOMPSON, E. M. 'The will and inventory of Robert Morton, A.D. 1486-1488', *J.B.A.A.* 33, 1877, 308-30. St. Olave's, London, and Standen, Hertfordshire.

Moscrofte
'A Newark surgeon's library', *N.G.* 1, 1895, 246-7. Nottinghamshire; will of Robert Moscrofte, 1606.

Mower
'Original documents', *Reliquary* 3, 1862-3, 226-8. Will and probate inventory of Rowland Mower of Eyam, Derbyshire, 1666.

Nevill
GUISEPPI, M. S. 'On the testament of Sir Hugh de Nevill, written at Acre, 1267', *Arch.* 56(2), 1899, 351-70

Ormond
See Butler.

Palmer
'The will of Richard Palmer of Naburn', *Reliquary* N.S. 8, 1894, 177-8. 1543.

Parker
SANDYS, WILLIAM. 'Copy of the inventory of Archbishop Parker's goods at the time of his death', *Arch.* 30, 1844, 1-30. 1575.

Perry
'Perry of Stafford', *N.G.* 1, 1895, 133-4. Will of Humphrey Perye, 1716.

Pierrepoint
'Pierrepoint of Holme Pierrepoint', *N.G.* 1, 1895, 169-70. Wills, 16-17th c.

Ponynges
GUNNER, WILLIAM H. 'The will of Luke de Ponynges, Lord St. John, of Basyng, from a copy in the register of William of

Wykeham', *A.J.* 11, 1854, 45-8. Hampshire; 1376.

Pullen
'Some colonial wills', *N.G.* 3, 1900, 82-3. Wills of Wm. Pullen of London and Jamaica, 1754; Richard Ware of Hull, Whitby and New Jersey, 1792.

Pulter
KERRY, CHARLES. 'The will of Alice Pulter, of St. Andrew's, Hitchin, Herts.', *Reliquary* N.S. 2, 1888, 30-31. 1458.

Pursglove
DUNKIN, E.H.W. 'Will of Bishop Robert Pursglove, a Derbyshire worthy', *Reliquary* 18, 1877-8, 223-4. 1580.

Ramsey
FAIRHOLT, F. W. 'On an inventory of the household goods of Sir Thomas Ramsey, Lord Mayor of London, 1577', *Arch.* 40(2) 1866, 311-42. Also includes his will, and extracts from his wife's.

Ratcliffe
'John Ratcliffe, Earl of Derwentwater', *N.G.* 2, 1896, 22. Will, 1731.

Redman
'Redman family', *N.G.* 5, 1902, 124. List of wills, from the Prerogative Court of Canterbury, 1383-1585.

Salvin
SALVIN, OSBERT. 'Sir Roger Salvin, 1420', *N.G.* 3, 1900, 147-9. Will.

Sanders
RICE, RICHARD GARRAWAY. 'The nuncupative will of Collingwood Sanders of Caldwell, Co. Derby', *Reliquary* 23, 1882-3, 63. 1653.

Selkirk
'Original document', *Reliquary* 4, 1863-4, 122-4. Will of Alexander Selkirk (Robinson Crusoe) of Largo, Fifeshire, 1717.

Smyth
'The will of John Smyth of Cottingham', *Reliquary* N.S. 7, 1893, 109-11. Yorkshire, 1504; includes brass.

Stanley
BURTT, JOSEPH. 'Original documents: will of Sir John Stanley, of Honford, Cheshire, dated 20 June, A.D. 1527', *A.J.* 25, 1868, 72-84.

Swynnerton
SWYNNERTON, C. 'Early Swynnerton wills at Lichfield, and other extracts', *Reliquary* 23, 1882-3, 39-44 & 223-4. Includes extracts from Church Lawton parish register, 16-17th c.
SWYNNERTON, C. 'Early Swynnerton wills at Lichfield, and other extracts', *Reliquary* 24, 1883-4, 34-5. Will of Humfrey Swynnerton, 1562.

Todd
PEACOCK, EDWARD. 'Robert Todd, of Bicker: a Lincolnshire yeoman of the XVI century', *Reliquary* 12, 1871-2, 148-51. Includes will and probate inventory, 1546.

Townley
'Townley of Townley, Co. Lancaster', *N.G.* 1, 1895, 122-4 & 159-60. Wills, 15-19th c.

Tymerman
'The will of Bernarde Tymerman of Hull, organ maker, 1535', *Reliquary* N.S. 8, 1894, 176-7.

Vaghan
WYNNE, W. WALKIN E. 'Inventory of the goods of Ievan ap Kenric Vaghan, dated A.D. 1361, 36 Edw. III, to which is appended his will', *A.J.* 22, 1865, 265-73.

Veer
HOPE, W. H. ST. JOHN. ' The last testament and inventory of John de Veer, 13th Earl of Oxford', *Arch.* 66, 1915, 275-348. 1509.

Venables
'Venables of Kinderton, Co. Chester', *N.G.* 1, 1895, 103-4. Will of Thomas Venables, 1604.

Walton
SIMPSON, JUSTIN. 'The will of the Rev. John Walton, B.D., Archdeacon of Derby, 1603', *Reliquary* 23, 1882-3, 110-17.

Ware
See Pullen.

Wharton
EVANS, JOAN. 'An inventory of Thomas Lord Wharton, 1568,' *A.J.* **102**, 1945, 134-50. Westmorland and Yorkshire.

Wicliffe
'Wicliffe of Wicliffe', *N.G.* **1**, 1895, 139. Will of Francis Wicliffe, prisoner of York Castle, 1610.

Wilmer
USSHER, RICHARD. 'Inventory of the goods of Sir Wm. Wilmer, Knt., preserved at Catton Hall, Derbyshire', *Reliquary* **21**, 1880-81, 176-8. Probate inventory, 1646.

E. INQUISITIONS POST MORTEM

1. By Place

Lincolnshire
BOYD, W. 'Lincolnshire inquisitions post mortem, temp Henry VII', *A.A.S.R.P.* **23**(1) 1895, 1-80.
MASSINGBERD, W.O. 'Early Lincolnshire inquisitions post mortem', *A.A.S.R.P.* **25**(1) 1899, 1-35.

Nottinghamshire
'Chancery inquisitiones post mortem, Hen. VIII, Nottinghamshire', *Reliquary* **24**, 1883-4, 14-16. List.

2. By family name

Dymoke
MASSINGBERD, W.O. 'Dymoke estates in Lincolnshire before 1650', *N.G.* **1**, 1895, 193-205. Inquisition post mortem, with extracts from the royalist composition papers, 1640.

Eyre
FURNESS, PETER. 'Extracts from an inquisition held at Belper, 1638', *Reliquary* **8**, 1867-8, 178-80. Inquisition post mortem on Thomas Eyre of Hassop, Derbyshire.

Linacre
'Deed relating to the Linacre family', *Reliquary* **10**, 1869-70, 244-5. Derbyshire; inquisition post mortem on Robert Linacre, c.1515.

Redman
'Redman evidences', *N.G.* **6**, 1903, 60-62. Lancashire, Carlisle and Yorkshire inquisitions post mortem.

5. PEDIGREE COLLECTIONS

WROTTESLEY, GEORGE. 'Pedigrees from the pleas [sic] rolls', *Reliquary* N.S. **1**, 1887, 159-65; **2**, 1888, 133-44. Many medieval pedigrees.

Cumberland
'Early Cumberland and Westmoreland pedigrees from the plea rolls', *N.G.* **4**, 1902, 138-9; **5**, 1903, 33-4. Burden, Raughton, Stirkland, Blenkhouse, Southayk, Gervaes, and Haltclough families; medieval.

Derbyshire
FLETCHER, W.G. DIMOCK. 'Pedigree showing the descent of Derbyshire peers from Henry VII, King of England', *Reliquary* **24**, 1883-4, 224(f). Cavendish, Hastings, Howard families, etc.
INCE, THOMAS. 'Derbyshire pedigrees', *Reliquary* **7**, 1866-7, 207-10. Savage of Castleton, 16-17th c., Needham of Thornsett and Snitterton, 16th c., Wendesley or Wensley, 15-17th c., Barley of Barley, otherwise Barlow, 15-17th c.
KIRKE, HENRY. 'Derbyshire pedigrees', *Reliquary* **7**, 1866-7, 17-31. *See* also 191. Derbyshire pedigrees from the visitations of other counties.
'Egerton Ms. 996. Derbyshire', *Reliquary,* **11**, 1870-71, 256. List of those whose right to bear arms was disclaimed at the heralds visitation of 1611.
KIRKE, HENRY. 'The ancient history of Chapel-en-le-Frith', *Reliquary* **8**, 1867-8, 227-40 & **9**, 1868-9, 17-28. Includes pedigrees of Ferrars, Earls of Derby; Bradshaw of Bradshaw; Browne of Marsh; Kyrke of Whitehough; Bagshawe of the Ridge; Barker of Malcalf; Bealott of Castlenaze; notes on deeds of Bagshawe and Browne; list of incumbents etc.

Lincolnshire

Stubton
ROYDS, E. 'Stubton strong room, stray notes (1st series): Heron and Crayle families; endowment of a London hospital', *A.A.S.R.P.* **38**, 1927, 1-55. Includes pedigrees of Heron, 17-19th c., Everingham, Sutthill and Constable, 14-17th c., Lely, 17-19th c., Crayle, 16-18th c., Bristowe, 17-18th c.

ROYDS, EDMUND. 'Stubton strong room: stray notes (2nd series). Moore and Knowles families; two sisters', *A.A.S.R.P.* **38**, 1927, 213-312. Includes pedigrees of Moore, 17-18th c., Knowles, 17-19th c., Gardiner, 17-19th c., Digby, 18-19th c., Steevens, 18-19th c.

Northamptonshire
Great Harrowden
SHARP, SAMUEL. 'Genealogical notes of some families connected with Northamptonshire, and in particular with Great Harrowden', *A.A.S.R.P.* **15**(1) 1879, 27-48. Especially Watson, Wentworth and Byng; includes pedigree of Wentworth, 16-19th c.

Staffordshire
'Harl. Ms. 1570: visitation of Staffordshire in 1583', *Reliquary* **11** 1870-71, 255-6. List of those disclaimed.

Westmorland
See Cumberland.

Yorkshire
'Pedigrees of the county families of Yorkshire', *Reliquary* **15**, 1874-5, 181-2. Book review.

6. FAMILY HISTORIES, etc.

Abney
'Abney of Willesley, Co. Derby', *Reliquary* **22**, 1881-2, 255. 15-17th c. pedigree.

Allen
See Baynbridge

Alleyne
FLETCHER, W.G. DIMOCK. 'Aleyne of Tideswell, Co. Derby', *Reliquary* **24**, 1883-4, 108-12. Includes parish register extracts from Loughborough, Leicestershire and Stratford upon Soar, Nottinghamshire.
FLETCHER, W.G. DIMOCK. 'Pedigree of Alleyne, of Derby and Loughborough', *Reliquary* **20**, 1879-80, 256. 18-19th c.
'Alleyne of Tideswell', *Reliquary* **14**, 1873, 64. See also **15**, 1874-5, 253. Derbyshire pedigree, 17th c.

'Descent of Alleyne from Edward I and (collaterally) from Archbishop Cranmer', *Reliquary* **24**, 1883-4, 106-7. 13-18th c., various counties.

Ashenhurst
SLEIGH, JOHN. 'Ashenhurst of Ashenhurst, and of Beard Hall', *Reliquary* **8**, 1867-8, 97-8. Staffordshire and Derbyshire, includes pedigree, 14-17th c.

Ashton
'Pedigree of Ashton and Shuttleworth of Hathersage', *Reliquary* **17**, 1876-7, 254-5. Derbyshire, 16-19th c.

Babington
CLARK, G. T. 'The Babingtons, Knights of St. John', *A.J.* **36**, 1879, 219-30. 16th c.
FLETCHER, W.G. DIMOCK 'Royal descent of Babington of Dethick, Co. Derby and Rothley Temple, Co. Leicester', *Reliquary* **21**, 1880-81, 237. 13-16th c.

Bagnall
SLEIGH, JOHN 'Bagnall of Bagnall, &c., Co. Stafford', *Reliquary* **10**, 1869-70, 111-12. Includes pedigree, 15-18th c.

Ball
LOWE, A.E. LAWSON. 'Ball of Tussingham and of Boughton', *Reliquary* **11**, 1870-71, 33-4. Cheshire; includes pedigree, 11-19th c.

Bampfylde
DYMOND, ROBERT 'Bampfylde House, Exeter', *A.J* **31**, 1874, 95-107. Includes pedigree of Bampfylde of Poltimore, Devon, 13-19th c.

Barritt
GIBBONS, THOMAS 'Thomas Barritt of Manchester', *Reliquary* **9**, 1868-9, 133-44. Includes pedigree.
WOOD, ALEXANDER B. 'Additional notes on Thomas Barritt of Manchester', *Reliquary* **12**, 1871-2, 205-8; **13**, 1872-3, 40-47. Includes pedigree, 18-19th c.

Bastard
COLVIN, H. M. 'The Bastards of Blandford: architects and master builders', *A.J.* **114**, 1947, 178-95. Includes pedigree, 18-19th c.

Bateman
JEWITT, LLEWELLYN. 'The late Thomas Bateman, esq., of Lomberdale House, and Middleton-by-Youlgreave', *Reliquary* 2, 1861-2, 87-97. Derbyshire; includes pedigree, 14-19th c.

Baynbridge
FLETCHER, W.G. DIMOCK. 'Heraldic grants to Derbyshire families', *Reliquary* 21, 1880-81, 240. Baynbridge and Allen families, 1582.

Bek
MASSINGBERD, W.O. 'An account of the family of Bek, of Lusby', *A.A.S.R.P.* 24(1) 1897, 33-56. Lincolnshire; includes pedigree, 12-14th c., and deed abstracts, etc.

Beresford
MARSHALL, GEORGE W. 'Beresford of Beresford', *Reliquary* 10, 1869-70, 64. Pedigree of London branch of the family, 17th c., additional to Sleigh's pedigree.
SLEIGH, JOHN 'Beresford of Beresford', *Reliquary* 9, 1868-9, 177-9. Beresford, Staffordshire, and Bentley, Derbyshire; includes pedigree, 11-19th c.

Bigges
BARNARD, E.A.B. 'The Bigges of Lenchwick and their tombs in Norton church, Evesham', *A.A.S.R.P.* 33(2), 1916, 396-411. Worcestershire; includes monumental inscriptions and wills, etc.

Bilbie
LOWE, A.E. LAWSON. 'Nottinghamshire pedigrees: Bilbie of Berry Hill', *Reliquary* 14, 1873-4, 111.

Blundell
LONGSTAFF, GEO BLUNDELL. 'Blundell of Liverpool', *N.G.* 6, 1903, 37-8 & 62-3. 17-19th c.

Booth
JEWITT, LLEWELLYN. 'The Booths or Bothes, Archbishop and Bishops, and the Derbyshire family to which they belonged', *Reliquary* 25, 1884-5, 33-40. 15-18th c.

Boothby
FLETCHER, W.G. DIMOCK. 'Royal descent of the family of Boothby, Baronets of Ashbourne, Co. Derby', *Reliquary* 21, 1880-81, 174-5. 13-18th c.

Bosville
See Hardwick.

Bourne
NODDER, JOSEPH 'Genealogical memoranda relating to the family of Bourne, of Ashover', *Reliquary* 15, 1874-5, 235-9. Derbyshire.

Bradshaw
BENNETT, WILLIAM. 'On Bradshaw Hall, near Chapel-en-le-Frith', *Reliquary* 2, 1861-2, 145-50. Derbyshire; Bradshaw family.
FURNESS, PETER 'On the Bradshaws and Staffords of Eyam, with a notice of the old hall', *Reliquary* 2, 1861-2, 219-26. Includes pedigrees.
'Some desultory jottings from the parish registers of Duffield, Co. Derby, relating to the family of Bradshawe, of that parish', *Reliquary* 23, 1882-3, 134-6. 17th c.

Braose
See De Albini.

Bray
'Family of Bray of Eyam', *Reliquary* 14, 1864-5, 64. Derbyshire; pedigree, 16th c?

Brereton
DWARRIS, FORTUNATUS, SIR. 'Observations upon the history of one of the old Cheshire families', *Arch.* 33, 1850, 55-83. Brereton family; medieval.

Brett
BUSHELL, W.D. 'The Bretts of Rotherby', *A.A.S.R.P.* 31(2), 1912, 471-94. Leicestershire; includes 16-17th c. pedigree.

Browne
BRADLEY, FREDERICK. 'Browne, of Lings, Derbyshire, claiming to be Viscount Montacute', *Reliquary* 5, 1864-5, 193-7.
KIRKE, HENRY 'Pedigree of Browne of Marsh, Co. Derby', *Reliquary* 11, 1870-71, 196. Medieval.
WRIGHT, GEORGE R. 'On Sir Anthony Browne, standard-bearer to King Henry VIII, and his descendants', *J.B.A.A* 23, 1867, 230-50.

'The family of Browne, of Etwall, in the county of Derby', *Reliquary* **24**, 1883-4, 71-2. Pedigree, 17-18th c.

Brus
See Meschines.

Brushfield
BRUSHFIELD, T.N. 'The origin of the surname of Brushfield', *Reliquary* **26**, 1885-6, 121-8. Derbyshire; medieval.

Bullock
JACKSON, CHARLES. 'Family of Bullock', *Reliquary* **20**, 1879-80, 31-2. Notes compiled c.1760; gives descent from 14th c. Of Ounston, Derbyshire.
See also Fromond.

Bunyan
BROWN, JOHN. 'Personal relics and recent memorials of John Bunyan', *A.A.S.R.P.* **16**(1) 1882, 88-97. Includes genealogical notes.

Burton
JEWITT, LL. 'The family of Burton of Dronfield and other places in Derbyshire', *Reliquary* **20**, 1879-80, 241-3. 13-17th c.

Calvert
I[NCE], T.N. 'Pedigree of Calvert, of Beely and Yeaveley, Co. Derby', *Reliquary* **14**, 1873-4, 84. 18-19th c.

Cantilupe
TREEN, A. EDWARD. 'Some historical notes on the parish of Barby, Northamptonshire, and the recent discoveries of fresco paintings on the church walls', *A.A.S.R.P.* **24**(2) 1898, 538-49. Includes pedigrees of Cantilupe, 13th c., and Zouche, 13-16th c.

Capell
DE COSSON, BARON. 'The Capells of Rayne Hall, Essex, with some notes on helmets formerly in Rayne church', *A.J* **40**, 1883, 64-79. 15-16th c.

Carill
See Worsley

Carlyle
CARLYLE, THOMAS. 'Short notices as to the early history of the family of Carlyle, which the Conqueror found in England, and a branch of which was ennobled in Scotland', *J.B.A.A* **9**, 1854, 174-81. Cumberland; includes pedigree, 11-17th c.

Carrier
See also Stoyte.

Castillion
'History of the family of Castiglione', *Arch.* **32**, 1847, 368-72. Berkshire; 16th c.

Cavendish
FLETCHER, W.G. DIMOCK. 'Royal descent of the ducal house of Cavendish', *Reliquary* **22**, 1881-2, 160(f). 12-18th c.
FOLJAMBE, C.G.S 'Chart showing the descent of the renaissance castle of Nottingham from its founder William Cavendish, Duke of Newcastle, in 1674, to the 7th and present Duke ...' *Reliquary* **21**, 1880-81, 184(f). Cavendish and Pelham Clinton family pedigrees.

Chambers
'Chambers of Derby', *Reliquary* **14**, 1873-4, 63. See also 126-7. Pedigree undated.

Chaworth
'Chaworth and Kniveton family alliance', *Reliquary* **22**, 1881-2, 126. 17th c., Surrey and Derbyshire.

Cheney
SLEIGH, JOHN. 'The Cheney family', *Reliquary* **11**, 1870-71, 115. Includes pedigrees of Cheney of Shurland, Kent, 15-17th c., and Cheney of Monyash, Ashford-in-the-Water, Derbyshire, 17-19th c.

Chetham
'Humphrey Chetham and the Chetham family', *Reliquary* **9**, 1868-9, 107-12 & 220-24.

Clare
ROUND, J. H. 'The family of Clare', *A.J.* **56**, 1899, 221-31. Suffolk; medieval.

Clarell
See Foljambe.

Clarke
'Clarke of Somersall, Chilcote, and Sutton, Co. Derby', *Reliquary* **22**, 1881-2, 126-7. Pedigree, 17-18th c.

Clay

CLAY, CHARLES. 'The family of Clay', *Reliquary* **10**, 1869-70, 145-6. See also 253-4. Derbyshire; includes pedigree, 17-19th c.

GILCHRIST, M 'The family of Clay, of North Wingfield, Crich, and other places, Co. Derby', *Reliquary* **25**, 1884-5, 51-2. Includes pedigree, 17-18th c.

INCE, T.N '[Clay of Hardstaff, pedigree]', *Reliquary* **11**, 1870-71, 64. Derbyshire; 18-19th c.

Claypole

ASTLEY, H. J. DUKINFIELD. 'Northborough church and manor house, in connection with Cromwell and the Claypoles', *J.B.A.A.* N.S. **5**, 1899, 122-40.

Clopton

HODGSON, ARTHUR. 'Clopton and the Cloptons', *J.B.A.A.* **32**, 1876, 238-42. 13-19th c.

Clyfton

SIMPSON, JUSTIN. 'The family of Clyfton, of Clyfton, juxta Nottingham', *Reliquary* **7**, 1866-7, 124-6.

Cockayne

'The Cockayne family', *Reliquary* **14**, 1873-4, 249-50. Derbyshire; book review.

Collin

LOWE, A.E. LAWSON. 'Nottinghamshire pedigrees: Collin of Nottingham and of Elton', *Reliquary* **15**, 1874-5, 162. 17-18th c.

Compton

COMPTON, C. H. 'Brambletye House', *J.B.A.A.* **41**, 1885, 372-7. Sussex; includes pedigree of Compton, 16-17th c.

SHIRLEY, EVELYN PHILIP. 'On the descent and arms of the house of Compton, of Compton Wyniate in the County of Warwick, Earls and Marquises of Northampton', *Arch.* **43**(1), 1871. 63-72. Medieval.

Conyers

SURTEES, F. R. 'Conyers of Sockburn', *J.B.A.A.* **43**, 1887, 149-54. Co. Durham.

Copledike

MASSINGBERD, W.O. 'Copledike of Harrington', *A.A.S.R.P.* **28**(1), 1905, 1-27. Lincolnshire; includes pedigree, 13-16th c.

Courtenay

OLIVER, GEORGE & JONES, PITMAN. 'Genealogy of the family of Courtenay, Barons of Okehampton and Earls of Devon', *A.J.* **10**, 1853, 53(f). Devon and Cornwall.

RUSPINI, FRANK ORDE 'The family of Courtenay, Earls of Devon', *Reliquary* **17**, 1876-7, 17-22, 97-104, 135-40 & 213-4.

Cromwell

See Claypole.

Dale

INCE, THOMAS NORRIS. 'Derbyshire pedigrees', *Reliquary* **7**, 1866-7, 181-4. Dale of Flagg, 17th c., Ince of Spinkhill, 14-17th c.

Danby

'The Danby family', *N.G.* **5**, 1902, 13-17. 16-17th c.

Darley

See Derley.

De Albini

DUDDING, REGINALD C. 'Ludborough', *A.A.S.R.P.* **42**(2), 1937, 189-220. Lincolnshire; includes pedigrees of De Albini, 11-13th c., Ross, 13-15th c., Braose, 13-15th c.

Degge

'Pedigree of the Degge family of Derby and of Stramshall, Co. Stafford', *Reliquary* **22**, 1881-2, 238-9.

De Montford

EVANS, F.W. 'The De Montfords of Beaudesert', *A.A.S.R.P.* **28**(1), 1905, 363-76. Worcestershire; 12-13th c.

Derley

'The family of Derley, of Derley, or Darley, Co. Derby', *Reliquary* **24**, 1883-4, 17. Brief medieval pedigree.

De Senlis

SERJEANTSON, R.M. 'The origin and history of the De Senlis family, grand butlers of France, and Earls of Northampton and

Huntingdon', *A.A.S.R.P.* 31(2), 1912, 503-18. Includes 12th c. pedigree.

Devey
See Hardwick.

Dodington
MARSHALL, GEORGE W. 'Genealogical notices of the family of Dodington, of Dodington, Co. Somerset', *Reliquary* 15, 1874-5, 86-90. Includes pedigree, 14-17th c., with will of George Dodington, 1618.
MARSHALL, G.W 'Pedigree of Marriott-Dodington of Horsington', *Reliquary* 13, 1872-3, 244-5. Somerset; 17-19th c.

Draper
'The family of Draper', *Reliquary* 15, 1874-5, 192. London; pedigree, 18-19th c.

Drayton
See Prayers.

Dymoke
See Hebden.

Edgcumbe
MOUNT EDGCUMBE, EARL OF. 'The history of the family of Mount Edgcumbe', *J.B.A.A.* 33, 1877, 145-22. Cornwall; Edgcumbe family, medieval.

Eyre
BEMROSE, WILLIAM. 'North Lees Hall, Derbyshire, and the family of Eyre, to whom it belonged', *Reliquary* 9, 1868-9, 201-6.
BENNETT, WILLIAM. 'The family of Eyre', *Reliquary* 3, 1862-3, 88-90. Derbyshire.
FURNESS, PETER. 'The family of Eyre of Hassop, in the county of Derby', *Reliquary* 10, 1869-70, 232-6. Includes pedigree, 15-19th c.
'The family of Eyre', *Reliquary* 26, 1885-6, 186. Brief pedigree, 17th c.

Fairfax
'Fairfax marriage licences at Worcester', *N.G.* 1, 1895, 95-6. 1697-1718.

Farnham
FLETCHER, W.G.D. 'Early history of the family of Farnham of Quorndon', *A.A.S.R.P.* 29(2), 1908, 585-600. Leicestershire; 13-16th c.
FLETCHER, W.G.D. 'The sequestration papers

of Edward Farnham of Quorndon', *A.A.S.R.P.* 28(2), 1906, 775-90. Leicestershire; 1645-6.

Farran
'Farran pedigree', *Reliquary* 12, 1871-2, 62(f). Various counties; Huguenot family, 18-19th c.

Ferne
'Ferne of Parwich, Co. Derby, and Crakemarsh, Co. Stafford', *Reliquary* 26, 1885-6, 32.

Ferrars
SLEIGH, JOHN. 'Ferrars, Earls Ferrars, Earls of Derby &c.', *Reliquary* 10, 1869-70, 225-6. Includes Ferrars family pedigree, 11-13th c.

Ferrers
PLANCHE, J. R. 'On the armorial bearings of Ferrers and Peverel', *J.B.A.A.* 7, 1852, 220-32. Medieval.
RICE, R. GARRAWAY. ' An illuminated pedigree of the Ferrers family, made in 1612, and presented to the Worshipful Company of Farriers in that year', *A.J.* 71, 1914, 261-74.

Fettiplace
PLANCHE, J. R. 'Genealogical notice of the family of Fettiplace', *J.B.A.A* 16, 1860, 201-4. Berkshire. Medieval; includes pedigree of Souza.

Finderne
F[LETCHER], W.G.D. 'Pedigree of Finderne', *Reliquary* 22, 1881-2, 64. Undated.
JEWITT, LLEWELLYN. 'Findern and the Fyndernes', *Reliquary* 3, 1862-3, 185-99. Derbyshire; includes Fynderne pedigree, 15-17th c.

Fitzgerald
PLANCHE, J. R 'On the family and connections of Robert Fitz Gerald, the domesday tenant of Corfe', *J.B.A.A.* 28, 1872, 113-22. Dorset.

Fitzwalter
PLANCHE, J. R. 'On the pedigree of Patrick Fitz-Walter, first Earl of Salisbury', *J.B.A.A.* 15, 1859, 26-46.

Fitzwilliam
HIGGINS, A. 'An illuminated and emblazoned copy of the statutes from Edward III to

Henry VI, illustrating the genealogy of the family of FitzWilliam of Mablethorpe, Co. Lincoln', *Arch.* 57, 1900, 1-10.
See also Foljambe.

Fletcher
See Jenkinson.

Foljambe
FLETCHER, W.G. DIMOCK. 'Royal descent of the family of Foljambe, (showing also the Clarell and Fitzwilliam connection)', *Reliquary* 20, 1879-80, 177-8. Medieval.
See also Loudham.

Frecheville
KIRKE, HENRY. 'The Frecheville letters', *Reliquary* 12, 1871-2, 27-37. Frecheville family, 17th c.

Freschville
SWIFT, W. 'Staveley Hall and its occupants', *Reliquary* 3, 1862-3, 149-58. See also 6, 1865-6, 248. Derbyshire; Freschville family.

Fromond
BIRCH, W. DE GRAY. 'Some private grants of armorial bearings', *J.B.A.A* 47, 1891, 323-6. Grants to Fromond of Strathfieldsay, 15th c., and Bullock of Berwick on Tweed 16th c.

Fynney
SLEIGH, JOHN. 'Fynney of Fynney', *Reliquary* 8, 1867-8, 458. Leek, Staffordshire; 12-19th c.

Garford
GARFORD, JOHN 'Garford of Steeton Hall, Yorkshire, and Garford, of Corby, Lincolnshire: Arthur Garforth, afterwards called Garford', *N.G* 4, 1901, 137. 17th c.

Garnon
'Pedigree of Garnon', *Reliquary* 10, 1869-70, 192. Nottinghamshire; c.15-17th c.

Garton
'The family of Garton', *Reliquary* 12, 1871-2, 245. Willougby on the Wolds, Nottinghamshire; 14-18th c.

Gell
SLEIGH, JOHN. 'Gell of Hopton', *Reliquary* 11, 1870-71, 225-6. Derbyshire; includes pedigree, 16-19th c.

Giffard
'The Giffards', *N.G.* 5, 1902, 94-5. See also 135. Review of Wrottesley, *The Giffards from the Conquest to the present time.* Staffordshire.

Gifford
PLANCHE, J. R. 'The family of the Giffords', *J.B.A.A.* 29, 1873, 58-68. Chillington, Somerset; medieval.

Gould
SLEIGH, JOHN. 'Gould, of Hanson-Grange', *Reliquary* 12, 1871-2, 45. Derbyshire; includes pedigree, 18-19th c.

Graham
BAIN, JOSEPH. 'The Grahams or Graemes of the Debateable Land; their traditional origin considered', *A.J.* 43, 1886, 116-23. Cumberland and Dumfrieshire.

Gratwick
'Pedigree of the family of Gratwick', *Reliquary* 18, 1877-8, 220(f). Sussex; 16-17th c.

Greatrakes
HAYMAN, SAMUEL. 'Notes on the family of Greatrakes, *Reliquary* 4, 1863-4, 81-96 & 220-36. See also 5, 1894-5, 94-104 & 183; 6, 1895-6, 183. Derbyshire.
LENIHAN, MAURICE. 'Further notes on the Greatrakes family', *Reliquary* 9, 1868-9, 162-6.

Greaves
I[NCE], T.N. 'Pedigree of Greaves, of the Greaves or Greves, Beely', *Reliquary* 14, 1873-4, 98. Derbyshire; 16th c.

Greystock
'The arms of Greystock', *N.G.* 5, 1902, 53. Greystock, Cumberland.

Hall
See Mortimer.

Halton
'Pedigree of Halton', *Reliquary* 5, 1864-5, 64. Lancashire, Derbyshire and Cumberland.

Hanson
HANSOM, JOSEPH. 'The roll of the freemen of York, and a pedigree of Hanson or

Hansome', *N.G.* **6**, 1903, 14-15. 16-18th c.

Hardinge
BRIGGS, JOHN JOSEPH. 'Memorials of King's Newton village, and its old hall', *Reliquary* **1**, 1860-61, 12-21. Hardinge family, of Melbourne, Derbyshire.

Hardman
L[OWE], A.E.L. 'Hardman family', *Reliquary* **15**, 1874-5, 190. See also 255. Manchester; pedigree, 18th c.

Hardwick
PRYCE, LEIGHTON. 'The family of Hardwicke, of Pattingham and Worfield', *Reliquary* **23**, 1882-3, 232-40. Staffordshire and Shropshire; 14-18th c.
SMITH, HUBERT. 'The families of Hardwick of Hardwick, and Devey of Hardwick, Copley and Clive', *Reliquary* **23**, 1882-3, 93-6. Extracts from court rolls of Pattingham, Shropshire; 15-17th c.
'Alliance of the Hardwick and Bosville families', *Reliquary* **24**, 1883-4, 10. Pedigree, 16th c.
'Some memorandums concerning the family of Hardwick, of Hardwick Co. Derby', *Reliquary* **22**, 1881-2, 241-3. 13-19th c.

Hastings
C., G.T. 'The rise and race of Hastings', *A.J.* **26**, 1869, 12-19, 121-36, & 236-57. Medieval; includes pedigrees.
FLETCHER, WM. GEO. DIMOCK. 'Extracts from Leicestershire registers relating to the Hastings family', *A.A.S.R.P.* **17**(2) 1884, 309-12. Includes will of Henry Hastings, Lord Loughborough, 1665, and list of other wills, etc.

Hatton
HELSBY, T. 'Baptisms, marriages and burials of the Hattons of Hatton, juxta Daresbury in Cheshire', *Reliquary* **15**, 1874-5, 221-4. *See also* Holdenby.

Havelock
'Notes on families bearing the surname Havelock', *N.G.* **4**, 1901, 150-3. Yorkshire and Essex; includes wills.

Haworth
HAWORTH, WILLIAM. 'The Haworths of Thurcroft, Co. Lancaster, and the descent of the Right Hon Sir Robert Peel, Bart; M.P., from the Haworths of Haworth in the same county', *Reliquary* **10**, 1877-8, 29-32. Includes pedigree, 17-19th c.

Hayman
HAYMAN, CANON. 'Memorials of the Hayman family and their armorial bearings', *Reliquary* **21**, 1880-81, 113-9 & 140-43.

Heathcote
JEWITT, LLEWELLYN. 'The Chesterfield bell founders and foundry: a notice of the Heathcote family', *Reliquary* **16**, 1875-6, 141-6.
'Heathcote of Chesterfield, Lord Mayor of London', *Reliquary* **22**, 1881-2, 156. Pedigree, 18th c.

Hebden
MADDISON, A. R. 'Breve ad inquirendum de bastardia et non bastardia dominae Katerinae Hebden', *A.J.* **43**, 1886, 75-7. Lincolnshire; includes notes on Hebden, Rye, Tempest and Dymoke families; medieval.

Hellesby
HELSBY, THOMAS. 'A Norman-French pedigree', *Reliquary* **9**, 1868-9, 231-7. Cheshire; Hellesby or Helsby family; includes pedigree, 11-16th c.

Heneage
MADDISON, A.R. 'The Heneage family', *A.A.S.R.P.* **25**(1) 1899, 36-47. Lincolnshire; includes notes on many deeds etc; 12-18th c.

Hilileigh
R., F. 'Hilileigh or Hillilee family', *N.G.* **5**, 1902, 75-6. Extracts from Halifax, Yorkshire, register, 16th c.

Hodgkinson
INCE, T.N. 'The family of Hodgkinson, of Overton Hall, in Ashover', *Reliquary* **12**, 1871-2, 254-5. Derbyshire; includes pedigree, 17-18th c.

Hodsoll
GREENSTREET, JAMES. 'The ancient Kent family of Hodsoll', *Reliquary* **18**, 1877-8, 217-20.
GREENSTREET, JAMES. 'Further notes on the ancient family of Hodsoll', *Reliquary* **19**, 1878-9, 161-4. Ightham, Kent; includes pedigrees, 16-19th c.

Holden
FLETCHER, W.G. DIMOCK. 'Royal descent of
Holden of Ashton, and Hurt, of Alderwasley,
Co. Derby', *Reliquary* 24, 1883-4, 80(f).
13-18th c.

Holdenby
HARTSHORNE, ALBERT. 'Holdenby,
Northamptonshire: its manors, church and
house', *A.J.* 65, 1908, 89-20. Includes brief
notes on memorials, and pedigree of
Holdenby and Hatton, 14-16th c.

Holland
HOLLAND, JOHN. 'The late Samuel Holland,
of Sheffield', *Reliquary* 11, 1870-71, 13-16.
Yorkshire; includes pedigree, 18-19th c.

Hope
JEWITT, LLEWELLYN. 'The destroyed church
of St. Giles, Normanton', *Reliquary* 2, 1861-2,
1-6. Derbyshire; includes pedigree of Hope.

Hurt
See Holden

Hutchinson
LOWE, A.E. LAWSON. 'Owthorpe and the
Hutchinsons', *Reliquary* 9, 1868-9, 239-42.
Nottinghamshire; includes pedigree,
c.15-18th c.

Hutton
'Hutton of Cartmel, Co. Lancaster', *N.G.* 5,
1902, 100-2. Includes parish register extracts.

Ince
See Dale.

Ireton
SLEIGH, JOHN. 'Ireton of Ireton, Co. Derby,
and Attenborough, Co. Notts', *Reliquary* 10,
1869-70, 169-70. See also 254, & 13, 1872-3,
189. Includes pedigree, medieval-18th c.

Jenkinson
FLETCHER, W.G. DIMOCK. 'Walton Hall, and
the families of Jenkinson and Fletcher, of
Walton, Co. Derby', *Reliquary* 20, 1879-90,
127-30. Includes pedigree, 17-18th c.

Keeling
F[LETCHER], W.G.D. 'The family of Keling or
Kelynge', *Reliquary* 24, 1883-4, 47-8.
Bedfordshire and London; 17th c. pedigree,
with wills.

F[LETCHER], W.G.D. 'The Keelinge family',
Reliquary 15, 1874-5, 239-40. Wolstanton,
Staffordshire; 16-17th c.
'Pedigree of the Keeling or Kelynge family',
Reliquary 14, 1873-4, 190. See also 15, 1874-5,
127; 16, 1875-6, 190-1. Various counties; 17-
19th c.

Keyworth
M[ARSHALL], G.W. 'Family of Keyworth',
Reliquary 9, 1868-9, 191-2. South Leverton
and Cottam, Nottinghamshire; includes
pedigree, 18th c.

Kinder
'Pedigree of Kinder', *Reliquary* 15, 1874-5,
167-8. See also 253; & 16, 1875-6, 63-4 & 125-
6. Medieval-17th c.

Kirke
SLEIGH, JOHN. 'Some account of the family
of Kirke, of Chapel-en-le-Frith, Derbyshire',
Reliquary 6, 1865-6, 213-9.

Kirkland
KIRKLAND, WALTER. 'Kirkland of Derbyshire', *Reliquary* 13, 1872-3, 219-23. Cumberland and Derbyshire; medieval-18th c.

Kniveton
HEATHER, W.M. 'Kniveton church, Co. Derby
and the Kniveton family', *Reliquary* 25,
1884-5, 149-53.
See also Chaworth.

Lander
'Pedigree of Lander', *Reliquary* 9, 1868-9,
254. Ashbourne, Derbyshire; 18-19th c.

Lechmere
WOOD, THOMAS W. 'The Lechmere family
and their ancient seat, with the family
pedigree', *A.A.S.R.P.* 20(1) 1889, 119-29. 13-
19th c.

Leekes
CLARK, C.H. 'The Leekes of Sutton',
Reliquary 10, 1869-70, 69-74. Derbyshire; 13-
17th c.

Lemon
FISHWICK, LT. COL. 'The Lemons of Preston',
Reliquary 17, 1876-7, 169-73. Lancashire;
17th c. Includes probate inventory of
Edmund Lemon, 1609.

Le Roter
See Rutter.

Lever
WALLIS, ALFRED. 'The diary of a London citizen in the seventeenth century', *Reliquary* N.S. 3, 1889, 90-98; 4, 1890, 135-41; 5, 1891, 13-20. Includes much genealogical information on the Lever family.

Linacre
INCE, THOMAS NORRIS. 'Derbyshire pedigrees: Linacre of Linacre Hall, near Chesterfield', *Reliquary* 9, 1868-9, 29. 15-16th c.

Lingen
BURGESS, J. TOM. 'The family of Lingen', *A.J.* 34, 1877, 373-85. Herefordshire.

Longsdon
SLEIGH, JOHN. 'The family of Longsdon, of Longsdon, in the county of Derby', *Reliquary* 9, 1868-9, 32. Includes pedigree, 13-19th c.

Loudham
FLETCHER, W.G. DIMOCK. 'The family of Foljambe', *Reliquary* 20, 1879-80, 160. Derbyshire. This is actually a pedigree of the Loudham family, 14-16th c., with whom the Foljambes were connected.

Lovet
See Prayers.

Lowe
L[OWE], A.E.L. 'Family of Lowe, of Owlgrave', *Reliquary* 10, 1869-70, 61. Derbyshire monumental inscription in Cheshire; 17th c.
LOWE, A.E. LAWSON 'The Lowes of Denby and Alderwasley', *Reliquary* 12, 1871-2, 113-4. Derbyshire; 15th c.
'Pedigree of the family of Lowe, or La Lowe, in the county of Chester, and of Alderwasley, Owlgrave, Hazlewood, Denby, ParkHall, and Locks Park, in the county of Derby, and elsewhere', *Reliquary* 11, 1870-71, 254. 15-19th c.

Lucy
COLLIER, J. PAYNE. 'Some information regarding the Lucies of Charlcote, the Shakespeares in and near Stratford-upon-Avon, and the property of William Shakespeare in Henley Street', *Arch.* 35, 1854, 18-22.

Lumley
PLANCHE, J. R 'On the portraits of the Lumley family at Lumley Castle, and their effigies at Chester-Le-Street', *J.B.A.A.* 22, 1866, 31-44. Co. Durham; 14-15th c.

Luttrell
See Mohun.

Lymerston
BAIGENT, FRANCIS JOSEPH. 'On the family of De Lymerston and its heiress, the founder of the Tichborne dole', *J.B.A.A.* 11, 1855, 277-302. Isle of Wight; medieval. Lymerston and Tichborne families.

Maddison
MADDISON, A.R. 'The making and unmaking of a Lincolnshire estate', *A.A.S.R.P.* 27(2), 1904, 337-77. Maddison family; includes pedigree, 14-19th c.

Malory
'[Pedigree of Malory, of Walton-on-the-Wolds, Leicestershire; 16th c.]', *Reliquary* 14, 1873-4, 256.

Mar
'Prophecy regarding the Earls of Mar', *Reliquary* 18, 1877-8, 221-3.

Marow
USSHER, RICHARD. 'Pedigree of Marow, of Berkswell, Co. Warwick, A.D. 1715', *Reliquary* 23, 1882-3, 50-51. 15-18th c.

Marriott
See also Dodington.

Marshall
MARSHALL, GEORGE W. 'The founder of Christ Church, Southwark', *Reliquary* 20, 1879-80, 169-71. John Marshall; includes genealogical notes on the Marshall family of Surrey, 16-17th c.
MARSHALL, GEORGE W. 'Notes on the families of Marshall, of Rampton and Tuxford, in the county of Notts., with extracts from the parish registers of those places', *Reliquary* 8, 1867-8, 27-32; 9, 1868-9, 69-72. Includes pedigrees, 17-19th c.

Massingberd

MADDISION, A.R. 'Family letters in the possession of Charles Massingberd-Mundy, esq., of Ormsby Hall', *A.A.S.R.P.* 23(2), 1896, 296-314. Lincolnshire; Massingberd family.

Mather

INCE, T.N. 'Pedigree of Mather of Derbyshire', *Reliquary* 9, 1868-9, 190-1. 18-19th c.
'The family of Mather of Derbyshire, Lancashire, &c.', *Reliquary* 15, 1874-5, 64. Pedigree, 17-18th c.

Meller

M[ARSHALL], G.W. 'The Meller family', *Reliquary* 7, 1866-7, 146. See also 255. Almondbury, Yorkshire; includes pedigree, 18-19th c.
M[ARSHALL], G.W. 'The Meller family', *Reliquary* 12, 1871-2, 168-72 & 216. Supplement to previous article; includes pedigree, 18th c., and parish register extracts, 16-18th c.

Meschines

SLEIGH, JOHN. 'Norman Earls Palatine of Cheshire', *Reliquary* 9, 1868-9, 79-80. Includes pedigree of Meschines, Brus, etc., medieval.

Middleton

INCE, T.N. 'Middleton of Wanesley, Notts., and Gratton, Co. Derby', *Reliquary* 12, 1871-2, 50. Pedigree, 17-18th c.

Mohun

LYTE, H. C. MAXWELL. 'Dunster and its lords', *A.J.* 37, 1880, 57-93, 155-79, 271-93 & 395-405; 38, 1881, 62-79 & 207-28. Mohun, Luttrell and Paganel families; includes pedigrees, 11-19th c., with extracts from accounts, etc., and list of the Priors of Dunster, Somerset.

Moigne

MADDISON, A. R. 'Original document: from a volume of brevia regia issued during the episcopate of John Bokingham, Bishop of Lincoln', *A.J.* 44, 1887, 403-4. Lincolnshire; includes pedigrees of Moigne, 14-16th c.

Montacute

See Browne

More

FOSS, EDWARD. 'The lineage of Sir Thomas More', *Arch.* 35, 1854, 27-33.

Mortimer

PLANCHE, J.R. 'On the genealogy and armorial bearings of the family of Mortimer', *J.B.A.A.* 24, 1868, 21-35. Medieval. 'Family jottings by a great-grandmother: the late Mrs. Marshall Hall', *Reliquary* 26, 1885-6, 89-95. Mortimer family, early 19th c.

Mundy

CLARK-MAXWELL, W. S. 'A grant of arms of the year 1510', *Arch.* 83, 1933, 167-70. To John Mundy of High Wycombe, Buckinghamshire.

Murgatroyd

C., W.F 'Murgatroyd of Murgatroyd, etc', *N.G.* 5, 1902, 45-6 & 116-8. Yorkshire; includes wills.

Neville

CRASTER, H.H.E. 'The origin of the Nevilles of Burreth', *A.A.S.R.P.* 37(2), 1925, 233-8. Lincolnshire; includes medieval pedigree.
NEVILE, CHARLES. 'Nevile of Thorney, Co. Notts', *N.G.* 1, 1895, 135-6.
PLANCHE, J. R. 'On the Norman ancestry of the Nevils, and the origin of the armorial bearings of the line of Raby', *J.B.A.A.* 22, 1866, 279-90. Cheshire.
PRITCHETT, J. P. 'The works of the Nevilles round Darlington', *J.B.A.A.* 43, 1887, 217-37. Includes genealogical notes, medieval.

Newcomen

FLETCHER, W.G.D. 'The family of Newcomen, of Saltfleetby', *A.A.S.R.P.* 24(1) 1897, 145-61. 13-18th c.
MADDISON, PREBENDARY. 'Notes on the Newcomen family', *A.A.S.R.P.* 24(1) 1897, 162-3.

Newton

FOSTER, C.W. 'Sir Isaac Newton's family', *A.A.S.R.P.* 39, 1928, 1-62. Lincolnshire; includes wills of Newton and Smith, and 16-17th c. pedigree of Newton.

Ollerenshaw

JEWITT, L. '[Ollerenshaw family]', *Reliquary* 11, 1870-71, 32. Derbyshire; 18-19th c.

Otter

LOWE, A.E.L. 'Pedigree of the family of Otter, of Welham, in the county of Nottingham', *Reliquary* 13, 1872-3, 248(f)

Overay

WEAVER, F.E. 'Thomas Overay, Precentor of Wells (1472-1493)', *Reliquary* N.S. 7, 1893, 218-22.

Paganel

See Mohun

Palmer

'The family of Palmer, of Sussex', *Reliquary* 9, 1868-9, 185-6. Book review.

Parker

J., C. 'The Right Honourable John Parker, and the family of Parker, of Norton, in the county of Derby', *Reliquary* 22, 1881-2, 139-44. 18-19th c.
PARKER, R. TOWNLEY. 'Evidences relating to the pedigree of Parker of Cuerden and Extwisle, Co. Lancaster', *Reliquary* 11, 1871, 161-2. Includes pedigree, 14-19th c.
SLEIGH, JOHN. 'Parker of Park Hall', *Reliquary* 10, 1869-70, 51-2. Norton Lees, Derbyshire, and Park Hall, Staffordshire; includes pedigree, c.14-19th c.
'The family of Parker, of Parwich, and other places in Co. Derby', *Reliquary* 25, 1884-5, 80. Pedigree, 18th c.
See also Stoyte

Pate

NORTH, THOMAS. 'Notes on the connection of the Pate family with Eye, Kettleby and Sysonby, Co. Leicester', *A.A.S.R.P.* 12(2) 1874, 275-82. Includes pedigree, 16-18th c., also pedigree of Smith of Chester, 15-17th c.

Peacock

'Note on family of Peacock of South Lincolnshire', *A.A.S.R.P.* 26(2), 1902, 394-7. Extracts from parish registers of Potter Hanworth and South Kyme, with memorial inscriptions.

Pelham Clinton

See Cavendish.

Percy

BAIN, J. 'The Percies in Scotland', *A.J.* 41, 1884, 335-41. Medieval.

Peverel

PLANCHE, J. R. 'On the family of Peverel of Nottingham as connected with the castle and the Earldom', *J.B.A.A.* 8, 1853, 194-208.
VICARS, A. 'Notes on an illuminated pedigree of the Peverell family and their descendants, in the possession of Mr. Hartshorne,' *A.J.* 49, 1892, 44-7.
See also Ferrers.

Pigot

LOWE, A.E. LAWSON. 'Nottinghamshire pedigrees: Pigot of Thrumpton', *Reliquary* 15, 1874-5, 15-16. 16-17th c.

Pilkington

See Stanley.

Pole

INCE, T.N. 'Pedigree of Pole, of Highedge (Heage), County of Derby', *Reliquary* 9, 1868-9, 218-9. 15-18th c.

Powle

BROWNE, A. L. 'The forbears of Sir Henry Powle of Shottesbrooke, speaker of the Convention Parliament and Master of the Rolls', *J.B.A.A.* 39, 1943, 362-81. Berkshire; includes pedigree 16-17th c., with will of Henry Powle, 1619/20.
See also Ferrers.

Powtrell

CARINGTON, RICHARD SMITH. 'Notes on the Leicestershire branch of the Powtrell family', *Reliquary* 24, 1883-4, 239-40. Medieval.
'Pedigree of Powtrell, of West Hallam, in the county of Derby', *Reliquary* 24, 1883-4, 157-60. 13-17th c.

Prayers

NICHOLS, JOHN GOUGH. 'Silver seal of Thomas de Prayers', *Arch.* 29, 1840, 405-7. Includes pedigrees of Prayers, Drayton, Lovet and Shirley, 12-16th c.
W., A. 'Certificate by the Black Prince regarding Thomas de Prayers, of Barthomley, Cheshire, dated 1343', *A.J.* 14, 1857, 349-52. Includes genealogical notes on Prayers family.

Pretye

'Family of Pretye', *Reliquary* 12, 1871-2, 124. Suffolk; pedigree written 1560.

Pytts

BALDWYN-CHILDE, MRS. 'Kyre Wyard, Worcs', *A.A.S.R.P.* **28**(2), 1906, 791-8. Pytts family, 16-18th c.

Redman

GREENWOOD, W. 'Further notes on early Redman history', *N.G.* **6**, 1903, 3-6. Cumberland and Westmorland; medieval.
GREENWOOD, W. 'The Redmans of Harewood Castle, Yorkshire', *N.G.* **5**, 1902, 54-68. 14-16th c., includes inquisitions post mortem, wills, etc.
GREENWOOD, W. 'The Redmaynes of Levens', *N.G.* **5**, 1902, 212. Medieval.
GREENWOOD, W. 'A sketch of the history of the Redmaynes of Levens, Harewood, and Thornton in Lonsdale', *N.G.* **4**, 1902, 105-12. Medieval.

Rhodes

'Rhodes of Lotherton, parish [of] Sherburn in Elmet', *N.G.* **2**, 1896, 176. Parish register extracts and monumental inscriptions, 17-18th c.

Richardson

'Some account of the probable ancestry of the Rev. Christopher Richardson, M.A., Trin. Coll. Camb., of Lascelles Hall, and rector of Kirkheaton, Yorks, 1646-61', *N.G.* **2**, 1896, 9-12. Includes folded pedigree, 16-19th c.

Riley

'Riley family', *Reliquary* **10**, 1869-70, 192. Pedigree, 16th c. County not given.

Roe

JEWITT, LLEWELLYN. 'A Derbyshire worthy: Charles Roe of Macclesfield', *Reliquary* **24**, 1883-4, 101-5. Cheshire; includes brief genealogical notes, 17-18th c.

Rokeby

BARTLETT, R. GROSVENOR. 'Rokeby family: Bible flyleaves', *N.G.* **3**, 1900, 37-8. Yorkshire; 17th c.
SIMPSON, JUSTIN. 'A Rokeby note from Rutland', *N.G.* **1**, 1895, 79. 17th c.

Rollesley

INCE, T.N. 'Pedigree of Rollesley or Rowlesley, of Little Rowsley, in Darley-in-the-Dale, Co. Derby', *Reliquary* **10**, 1869-70, 167-8. 13-17th c.

Ross

See De Albini.

Rudyerd

SLEIGH, JOHN. 'Rudyerd of Rudyerd', *Reliquary* **7**, 1866-7, 211-19. See also **8**, 1867-8, 62. Staffordshire; 11-19th c.

Russell

FRYER, ALFRED C. 'A monumental effigy of Bridget, Countess of Bedford', *A.J.* **73**, 1916, 212-6. Chenies, Buckinghamshire.

Rutter

HELSBY, T. 'Le Roter, or Rutter, of Kingsley, Co. Pal. Chester', *Reliquary* **12**, 1871-2, 129-38 & 229-38. Kingsley, in Frodsham, and Norlay, Cheshire; Quinton, Gloucestershire; New Malton, Yorkshire. Includes pedigrees, 16-19th c.

Rye

See Hebden

Ryther

BROWN, W. 'A Yorkshire knight and his wife in the fifteenth century', *Reliquary* **5**, 1891, 112-3. Ryther family.

Sackville

ROUND, J. H. 'The Essex Sackvilles', *A.J.* **64** 1907, 217-26. Medieval.

Sanders

SLEIGH, JOHN. 'The family of Sanders of Lullington, Caldwell, Ireton, &c., Co. Derby', *Reliquary* **11**, 1870-71, 166. Includes pedigree, 15-19th c.

Saundby

CARTER, W.F. 'Saundby of Saundby, Co. Notts', *N.G.* **1**, 1895, 88-91. Includes 18th c. pedigree and wills.

Savile

BAILEY, W.H. 'Notes on the Saviles, lords of the manor of Blaby in the county of Leicestershire', *A.A.S.R.P.* **32**(1), 1913, 229-34. Includes 15-17th c. pedigree.
I[NCE], T.N. 'Pedigree of Savile, of Hill Top in Beeley', *Reliquary* **14**, 1873-4, 102.

Sawyer
BULL, F.W. 'The Sawyers of Kettering', *A.A.S.R.P.* **28**(1), 1905, 102-12. Northamptonshire; 16-18th c.

Scatcherd
'Scatcherd of Bishop Monkton', *N.G.* **1**, 1895, 142. Yorkshire; pedigree, 17-18th c.

Scrope
RAINE, J. 'The Scropes in connection with York Minster', *A.A.S.R.P.* **6**(1) 1861, 46-51. 15th c.

Shakespeare
See Lucy

Shepley
LUMB, G.D. 'Shepley pedigree', *N.G.* **2**, 1896, 199-205. Includes folded pedigree, 18-19th c., wills, monumental inscriptions, extracts from a family bible and from newspapers, etc.

Shireburne
COX, J. C. 'Some notes on the family of Shireburne of Stonyhurst', *A.J.* **56**, 1899, 51-68. Lancashire; 17-18th c.

Shirley
KIRKE, HENRY. 'The manor of Shirley', *Reliquary* **9**, 1868-9, 188-90. Derbyshire; Shirley family, including medieval pedigree. *See also* Prayers.

Shuttleworth
See Ashton.

Sinclair
'Genealogy of the Sinclairs of Ireland', *Reliquary* **9**, 1868-9, 187. Book review.

Sleigh
EDWYN-COLE, JAMES. 'Genealogy of Sleigh, of Derbyshire', *Reliquary* **7**, 1866-7, 147-51.

Smith
HUNT, ALFRED. 'A few notes concerning the founder of Lincoln Christ's Hospital (or the Old Blue Coat School), Richard Smith, 1530-1602', *A.A.S.R.P.* **35**(2), 1920, 243-6. Includes pedigree of Smith of London and Welton, Lincolnshire; 16-17th c.
See also Newton and Pate.

Soley
MARSHALL, GEORGE W. 'Pedigree of Soley, of Orleton and Worcester', *Reliquary* **18**, 1877-8, 207-8. Pedigree, 17th c., with extracts from the parish registers of Eastham, Worcestershire; 16-18th c.
MARSHALL, GEORGE W. 'Further notes on the family of Soley', *Reliquary* **19**, 1878-9, 28. Extracts from parish registers of Warndon, Claines, etc., Worcestershire; 16-17th c.

Somersall
'Somersall family', *Reliquary* **14**, 1873-4, 256. Walton-on-the-Wolds, Leicestershire; pedigree, 16th c.

Somerset
W., W. S. 'Note as to the Henry Lord Herbert named in the will of the Princess Katherine, Countess of Devon', *A.J.* **10**, 1853, 240. 16th c., Somerset family.

Southeran
'The Southeran family', *Reliquary* **15**, 1874-5, 55-6. Co. Durham, Yorkshire and Northumberland; book review.

Souza
See Fettiplace.

Stafford
'The Stafford family of Eyam, Chapel-en-le-Frith, Manchester, etc', *Reliquary* **16**, 1875-6, 192. Derbyshire and Lancashire; includes pedigree, 18th c.
See also Bradshaw.

Stanley
PLANCHE, J. R. 'On the Stanley Crest', *J.B.A.A.* **6**, 1851, 199-209. Includes pedigree of Pilkington, 14th c., and genealogical notes on Stanley.
S., E. 'Original documents: the formal decree of divorce of Sir John Stanley, of Honford, and Margaret, his wife, dated June 25, 1528', *A.J.* **25**, 1868, 233-41. Cheshire; on his becoming a monk.

Stanton
ESDAILE, ARUNDELL, MRS. 'The Stantons of Holborn', *A.J.* **85**, 1928, 149-69. 17-18th c., monumental sculptors.

Stoyte
INCE, T.N. 'Pedigrees of several vicars and

other public men of Wirksworth', *Reliquary* **12**, 1871-2, 46-7. Derbyshire; pedigrees of Stoyte, Parker and Carrier, 16-18th c.

Sudeley

WEST, STANLEY E. 'Griff manor house (Sudeley Castle), Warwickshire', *J.B.A.A.* 3rd series **31**, 1968, 76-101. Sudeley family; includes pedigree, 15-16th c.

Sumner

FISHWICK, MAJOR. 'On genealogical information contained in old bibles', *Reliquary* **9**, 1868-9, 30-1. Sumner family; 16-17th c.

Swynnerton

SWYNNERTON, CHARLES. 'Concluding notes on the family of Swynnerton of Swynnerton and other places in Co. Stafford', *Reliquary* **22**, 1881-2, 15-16.

SWYNNERTON, CHARLES. 'Further notes on the family of Swynnerton of Swynnerton and other places in the county of Stafford', *Reliquary* **19**, 1878-9, 44-6, 99-102 & 205-8; **20**, 1879-80, 21-5 & 104-8; **21**, 1880-81, 34-8 & 97-101.

SWYNNERTON, CHARLES. 'Notes on the family of Swynnerton of Swynnerton and other places in Co. Stafford', *Reliquary* **18**, 1877-8, 167-9.

SWYNNERTON, C. 'On the armorial ensigns of the Swynnertons', *Reliquary* **20**, 1879-80, 223-8.

SWYNNERTON, C. 'On the first five descents in the pedigree of Swynnerton, Co. Stafford', *Reliquary* **22**, 1881-2, 152-6. Medieval.

SWYNNERTON, C. 'The parish registers of Whitmore, Co. Stafford so far as they relate to the family of Swynnerton', *Reliquary* **22**, 1881-2, 223-4. 16-17th c.

SWYNNERTON, C. 'The Swynnertons of Eccleshall', *Reliquary* **21**, 1880-81, 169-73. Staffordshire; 13-17th c.

SWYNNERTON, C. 'The Swynnertons of Salem, Massachusetts, United States', *Reliquary* **23**, 1882-3, 115-6. 17-18th c.

'A pedigree showing the probable connection of the Swynnertons of Swynnerton, of Hilton, and of Eccleshall, 14th and 15th centuries', *Reliquary* **21**, 1880-81, 238-9. Staffordshire; 13-16th c.

Syston

SYSTON, ED. J. 'The Syston or Syson family', *Reliquary* **12**, 1871-2, 124. See also **14**, 1873-4,

189. Walton on the Wolds, Leicestershire; letter to the editor, giving pedigree, 16-17th c.

'The family of Syerson, Syerston, Syston, Syson, Sisson or Sison, alias Barton of Wollaton, Co. Notts', *Reliquary* **10**, 1869-70, 191. Pedigree, 17-19th

V., Q.P. 'The Syston family', *Reliquary* **8**, 1867-8, 191. Leicestershire; includes pedigree, 16-17th c.

Talbot

WOOD, WILLIAM. 'The Talbots of Eyam', *Reliquary* **5**, 1864-5, 148-51. Derbyshire.

Tames

HOLT, HENRY F. 'The Tames of Fairford', *J.B.A.A.* **27**, 1871, 110-48. Gloucestershire; includes pedigree, 15-16th c.

Tarbock

HELSBY, T. 'Extracts from the registers and transcripts of registers of parish churches of Huyton and Prescot, Co. Lancaster, relating to the family of Tarbock of Tarbock', *Reliquary* **12**, 1871-2, 23-6.

Tempest

TEMPEST, E. BLANCHE. 'Tempest of Holmeside, Co. Durham', *N.G.* **1**, 1895, 5-14. 14-16th c.
See also Hebden.

Thornhaugh

MARSHALL, GEORGE W. 'Grant of crest to John Thornhagh of Fenton, Co. Nottingham', *Reliquary* **18**, 1877-8, 15-16.

SAVILE, CECIL G. 'The Nottinghamshire family of Thornhaugh from the original ms of 1683', *Reliquary* **16**, 1875-6, 41-4, 103-6 & 197-204; **17**, 1876-7, 235-8.

Tichborne

See Lymerston.

Timperley

CORDER, J. SHEWELL. 'Hintlesham Hall', *J.B.A.A.* N.S. **34**, 1928, 87-95. Suffolk; Timperley family, 15-16th c.

Torbock

HELSBY, THOMAS. 'Torbock of Torbock, Co. Lancr', *Reliquary* **10**, 1869-70, 171-5 & 227-31; **11**, 1870-71, 35-9 & 97-102. Includes pedigree, medieval-18th c.

43

Tournay

MADDISON, A.R. 'The Tournays of Caenby', *A.A.S.R.P.* **29**(1), 1907, 1-42. Lincolnshire; includes pedigree, 14-18th c., deed abstracts, rentals, etc.

Tyrell

SEWELL, W. H. 'Sir James Tyrell's Chapel at Gipping, Suffolk', *A.J.* **28**, 1871, 23-33. Includes pedigree, 15-16th c.

Valoigne

GREENSTREET, JAMES. 'The Kent branch of the ancient family of Valoignes', *Reliquary* **16**, 1875-6, 97-102.

Verdon

SLEIGH, JOHN. 'Verdon of Alton', *Reliquary* **8**, 1867-8, 145. Staffordshire; includes pedigree, 11-15th c.

Vere

NICHOLS, JOHN GOUGH. 'On the descent of the Earldom of Oxford', *A.J.* **9**, 1852, 17-29. Vere family, 12-17th c.

Vernon

CARRINGTON, W. A. 'On the family and record history of Haddon', *J.B.A.A.* N.S. **6**, 1900, 140-58. Derbyshire; Vernon family, medieval.

FLETCHER, W.G. DIMOCK. 'Royal descent of the noble family of Vernon of Co. Derby', *Reliquary* **21**, 1880-81, 126(f). 13-17th c.

Warrene

COAD, J. G., & STREETON, A. D. F. 'Excavations at Castle Acre Castle, Norfolk, 1972-77: country house and castle of the Norman Earls of Surrey', *A.J.* **139**, 1982, 138-301. Includes notes on the Warrenes, Earls of Surrey.

STAPLETON, THOMAS. 'Observations in disproof of the pretended marriage of William de Warren, Earl of Surrey, with a daughter begotten of Matildis, daughter of Baldwin, Comte of Flanders, by William the Conquerer, and illustrative of the origin and early history of the family in Normandy', *A.J.* **3**, 1846, 1-26.

Washington

'Washingtons from Kirkby Lonsdale register', *N.G.* **5**, 1902, 89. Westmorland.

Watson

WINCKLEY, S.T. 'Royalist papers relating to the sequestration of the estates of Sir Lewis Watson, Knight and baronet, afterwards first Baron Rockingham of Rockingham Castle, during the civil wars in England', *A.A.S.R.P.* **25**(2), 1900, 371-404.

Webster

FISHWICK, LT. COL. 'The Websters of Hargreave', *Reliquary* **12**, 1871-2, 201-4. Lancashire; 15-19th c.

Whitaker

HELSBY, T. 'Whitaker of Whitaker, Holme, and Healey, County of Lancaster', *Reliquary* **12**, 1871-2, 81-4. Includes pedigree, 10-19th c.

White

INCE, T.N. 'Pedigree of White, of Ashford-in-the-Water', *Reliquary* **13**, 1872-3, 252-3. Derbyshire; 18-19th c.

INCE, T.N. 'Pedigree of White, of Great Longstone, Co. Derby', *Reliquary* **13**, 1872-3, 254. 18th c.

LEGGE, W. HENEAGE. 'Delves House, Ringmer; with some account of Gilbert White and his relatives there residing', *Reliquary and illustrated archaeologist*, N.S. **6**, 1900, 1-14. Sussex.

Wigley

'Pedigree of Wigley, of Gatehouse, Wirksworth', *Reliquary* **12**, 1871-2, 48-9. Derbyshire; 15-17th c.

'Pedigree of Wigley, of Wigwell Grange', *Reliquary* **12**, 1871-2, 16. Derbyshire; 17-18th c.

Woodcock

HELSBY, T. 'Genealogy of Woodcock, Co. Lancaster', *Reliquary* **14**, 1873-4, 146-8. Includes pedigree, medieval-16th c.

LOWE, A.E. LAWSON. 'The family of Woodcock, of Woodcock Hall', *Reliquary* **15**, 1874-5, 13-15. Lancashire; includes pedigree, 18-19th c.

Worsley
SLEIGH, JOHN. 'Worsley, of Platt, Co. Pal. Lanc', *Reliquary* 11, 1870-71, 40-42. Includes pedigree of Carill-Worsley of Platt Hall, Lancashire, and Winster, Derbyshire.

Wren
REDFARN, W.B. 'The mitre and crozier of Bishop Wren at Pembroke College, Cambridge', *Reliquary* 22, 1881-2, 65-8. Includes pedigree, 17th c.

Wright
BEMROSE, F.W. 'The family of Wright, of Derbyshire and Staffordshire', *Reliquary* 13, 1872-3, 176. Includes pedigree, 17-19th c.

Wylde
BULLOCK, L. 'Wylde of Worcestershire', *A.A.S.R.P.* 29(2), 1908, 617-44.

Yelverton
GOTCH, J.A. 'Easton Mauduit, the home of the Yelvertons', *A.A.S.R.P.* 36(1), 1921, 95-102. Northamptonshire; 17-18th c.

Zouche
See Cantilupe.

7. DESCENTS OF MEDIEVAL LORDSHIPS: DUKEDOMS, EARLDOMS, ETC.

CAULDWELL, RALPH. 'On the descent of titles of honour, particularly baronies, through the female line, transcribed from a ms. of Mr. Sayntlowe Kniveton', *Arch.* 3, 1775, 285-302. Includes many baronial pedigrees.

Belvoir, Lords of
CARRINGTON, W. A. 'The early lords of Belvoir', *J.B.A.A.* N.S. 7, 1901, 299-326; 8, 1902, 17-38. Todeni, Albini and Ros families, 11-17th c. Includes inquisition post mortem for William de Ros, 1352. This article is corrected in: BROWNE, A. L. 'The Honour of Belvoir', *J.B.A.A.* N.S. 38, 1932, 129-32.

Chester, Earls of
PLANCHE, J. R. 'On the seals of the Earls of Chester', *J.B.A.A.* 5, 1850, 235-52. Includes genealogical notes.

Cornwall, Earls and Dukes of
PLANCHE, J. R. 'The Earls of Cornwall', *J.B.A.A.* 33, 1877, 46-59.
TUCKER, STEPHEN I. 'The Duchy and Dukes of Cornwall', *J.B.A.A.* 33, 1877, 60-67.

East Anglia, Earls of
PLANCHE, J. R. 'The Earls of East Anglia', *J.B.A.A.* 21, 1865, 91-103. Bigot family.

Galloway, Lords of
RIDDELL, ROBERT. 'An account of the ancient lordship of Galloway, from the earliest period to the year 1655, when it was annexed to the Crown of Scotland', *Arch.* 9, 1789, 49-50. Includes pedigree showing relationship of Quincy, Baliol, Cuming and Douglas; medieval.

Glamorgan, Lords of
CLARK, G. T. 'The Land of Morgan: the chief lords', *A.J.* 35, 1878, 1-18. Descent of the lordship; medieval.

Gloucester, Earls of
CLARK, G.T. 'The land of Morgan, pt.3: the Earls of Gloucester', *A.J.* 35, 1878, 313-38.
PLANCHE, J. R. 'The Norman Earls of Gloucester', *J.B.A.A.* 25, 1869, 26-41. With comment by Sir P. Stafford Carey.

Hereford, Earls of
PLANCHE, J. R. 'The genealogy and armorial bearing of the Earls of Hereford', *J.B.A.A.* 27, 1871, 179-91.

Holderness, Lords of
PLANCHE, J. R. 'The early lords of Holderness', *J.B.A.A.* 30, 1874, 121-9.

Isle of Wight, Lords of
PLANCHE, JAMES ROBINSON. 'On the lords of the Isle of Wight', *J.B.A.A.* 11, 1855, 213-26. Medieval; Fitz Osborne, Breteuil, Redvers, Vernon, Fortibus, Montacute, and Wideville families.

Kent, Earls of
PLANCHE, J. R. 'Genealogical and heraldic notices of the Earls of Kent', *J.B.A.A.* 9, 1854, 361-75.

Lincoln, Earls of
HILL, J.W.F. 'Lincoln Castle: the constables and the guard', *A.A.S.R.P.* **40** 1930, 1-14. Includes the descent of the Earldom of Lincoln, 11-14th c.

Northumbria, Palatinates of
PACE, WILLIAM. 'Some remarks on the Northumbrian palatinates and regalities', *Arch.* **51**, 1888, 143-55. Includes pedigree of the house of Bamburgh, 10-13th c.

Somerset, Dukes and Earls of
PLANCHE, J. R. 'On the succession and armorial bearings of the Earls and Dukes of Somerset', *J.B.A.A.* **12**, 1856, 312-28. Mohun, Beaufort, Seymour, etc., medieval.

Strigul, Earls of
PLANCHE, J. R. 'On the Earls of Strigul and Lords of Chepstow', *J.B.A.A.* **10**, 1855, 265-74. Fitz Gilbert; medieval.

Sussex, Earls of
PLANCHE, J. R. 'The Earls of Sussex', *J.B.A.A.* **23**, 1867, 21-33. Montgomery, de Albini, and Warren families; medieval.

Worcester, Earls of
PLANCHE, J. R. 'The Earls of Worcester and Hertford', *J.B.A.A.* **26**, 1870, 149-60.

8. MANORS

Works relating to deeds, accounts, and other manorial documents are also listed in section 9.

A. MANORIAL RECORDS

Buckinghamshire

Aylesbury
PARKER, JOHN. 'The manor of Aylesbury', *Arch.* **50**(1), 1887, 81-103. Includes many names, also medieval pedigree showing descent of the manor through Boteler and Bullen.

Derbyshire

INCE, T.N. 'Wirksworth, Bonsall, Brassington, and Ireton Wood: certain copy holds confirmed', *Reliquary* **12**, 1871-2, 125-6, 189-

91 & 253-4. Rental, listing copy holders, 1620.

Ounston
JACKSON, CHARLES. 'Notes from court papers for the manor of Ounston, or Unston, in Derbyshire', *Reliquary* **20**, 1879-80, 246. Includes list of deceased tenants and heirs, 1683.

Hampshire

Meonstoke
KIRBY, T. F. 'Charters of the manor of Meonstoke', *Arch.* **57**(2), 1901, 285-94. Medieval.

Ropley
KIRBY, T. F. 'Charters of the manor of Ropley, Hants', *Arch.* **58**, 1902, 227-36. Medieval; includes pedigrees of Gerveys and Tyghale.

Lancashire

Manchester
EARWAKER, J. P. 'The early deeds relating to the manor of Manchester, now in the possession of the Corporation of that city', *J.B.A.A.* N.S. **1**, 1895, 49-57. Medieval.

Leicestershire

Lutterworth
CLARK, GEO. T. 'Schedule of a parcel of the lands of Henry, Duke of Suffolk, within the manor of Lutterworth, farmed out to various tenants at a specified rental', *A.J.* **48**, 1891, 190-2. Gives names of tenants, 16th c.

Rothley
CLARKE, GEO. THOMAS. 'The custumary of the manor and soke of Rothley, in the county of Leicester', *Arch.* **47**, 1883, 89-130. 13th c. Includes names.

Withcote
FARNHAM, G., & THOMPSON, A. HAMILTON. 'Notes on the history of the manor of Withcote', *A.A.S.R.P.* **36**(1), 1921, 127-82. Includes wills of Roger Radclyff, 1536, and Henry Pole, 1558; inquisitions post mortem for Henry Smith, 1620, and Henry Smith, 1622; pedigrees of Smyth, 16-17th c., Palmer, 15-16th c., Hotoft, 13th c., Kirkeby, 13-15th c., Ward, 14-15th c., poll tax return, 1381; list of rectors.

Lincolnshire

Addlethorpe
See Ingoldmells.

Bottesford
PEACOCK, EDWARD. 'Notes from the records of the manor of Bottesford, Lincolnshire', *Arch.* 50(2), 1887, 371-82. Includes many names from 16th c. court rolls.

Epworth
JACKSON, CHARLES. 'Notes from the court rolls of the manor of Epworth in the county of Lincoln', *Reliquary* 23, 1882-3, 44-8, 89-92 & 174-6. 16-18th c.

Gosberton
'Gosberton court rolls', *N.G.* 2, 1896, 85-6. Brief medieval extracts.

Hibaldstow
PEACOCK, E. 'The court rolls of the manor of Hibbaldstow', *A.J.* 44, 1887, 278-88. 15-16th c.

Ingoldmells
MADDISON, A.R. 'Manor of Ingoldmells-cum-Addlethorpe court rolls', *A.A.S.R.P.* 21, 1891, 176-90. Medieval.

Langton
MASSINGBERD, W.O. 'Some ancient records relating to the manor of Langton and its lords', *A.A.S.R.P.* 22(2) 1894, 157-73. Includes inquisitions post mortem of Langton family, various lists of fees, extents, deeds, etc.

Lincoln
HILL, J.W.F. 'The manor of Hungate or Beaumont Fee, in the city of Lincoln', *A.A.S.R.P.* 38, 1927, 175-208. Includes transcripts of many lists of names from manorial records, 17-18th c.

Somersby
MASSINGBERD, W.O. 'The manors of Somersby and Tetford', *A.A.S.R.P.* 23(2), 1896, 253-9. Deeds and inquisitions post mortem, mainly relating to the Thimbleby family.

Stallingborough
MADDISON, A.R. 'The manor of Stallingborough', *A.A.S.R.P.* 23(2) 1896, 274-89. Rental, 1351.

Stow
MASSINGBERD, W.O. 'Survey of the manor of Stow, A.D. 1283', *A.A.S.R.P.* 24(2) 1898, 299-347.

Tetford
See Somersby.

London and Middlesex

Savoy
WALTON, WILLIAM. 'Accompts of the manor of Savoy, temp. Richard II', *Arch.* 24, 1832, 299-316. Includes names.

Northamptonshire

Higham Ferrers
SERJEANTSON, R.M. 'Court rolls of Higham Ferrers', *A.A.S.R.P.* 33(1), 1915, 95-141; 33(2), 1916, 326-69 & 34(1), 1917, 47-102. Not a transcript, but includes many names.

Oundle
JEAYES, I.H. 'On the compotus rolls of the manor of Oundle, in the possession of the Association', *J.B.A.A.* 34, 1878, 384-90.

Towcester
'A court roll of the manor of Towcester, 1510-11', *Reliquary* N.S. 8, 1894, 169-73.

Northumberland

Hexham
'Manor rolls of Hexham, Co. Northumberland', *N.G.* 1, 1895, 39-41. Brief description and list, with list of surnames occurring.

Oxfordshire

Bampton
WILLIAMS, BENJAMIN. 'Additional remarks on the hide of land, and on some ancient manorial customs in Oxfordshire', *Arch.* 35, 1854, 470-74. Includes customary of Bampton, with names of 'substantiall inhabitants'.

Suffolk

Cavendish
RUGGLES, THOMAS. 'Notices of the manor of Cavendish in Suffolk, and of the Cavendish family while possessed of that manor', *Arch.* 11, 1794, 50-62. Includes pedigrees of Gernon and Cavendish, 14-16th c.

Wiltshire

Durrington

KIRBY, T. F. 'Records of the manor of
Durrington, Wilts', *Arch.* **59**, 1904, 75-82.
Medieval deeds, etc.

Yorkshire

Dunnington

'Dunnington, Co. York, court rolls', *N.G.* **5**,
1902, 120-24. Abstracts, 1606-40.

Wakefield

'Heriots, &c., in the Wakefield manor rolls',
N.G., **3**, 1900, 169-72; **4**, 1901, 7-12, 57-65 &
113-5; **5**, 1902, 20-23, 69-74 & 130-35; **6**, 1903,
42-8 & 52-9. 1416-27 and 1500-1560
'Wakefield manor rolls: a great court baron',
N.G. **6**, 1903, 49-51. General discussion.
'Wakefield manor rolls: a great court leet',
N.G. **5**, 1902, 125-9. General discussion.

B. MANORIAL DESCENTS, etc.

Derbyshire

Haddon Hall

DUESBURY, HENRY. 'Haddon Hall', *J.B.A.A.*
7, 1851, 284-95. Includes notes on lords,
including Avenall, Basset, Vernon, Peverell
and Manners.

Essex

Bacons and Great Tey

ASTLE, THOMAS. 'On the tenures, customs,
&c., of his manor of Great Tey', *Arch.* **12**,
1796, 24-40. Includes descent of Great Tey
and Bacons manors, and of various fiefs
within the manor.

Leicestershire

Hamilton

KENDALL, G.E. 'The town of Hamilton,
Leics., and its ancient lords: a sketch from
the plea rolls and other sources', *A.A.S.R.P.*
35(2), 1920, 323-56. Descent through
Hamilton, Somerville and Willoughby;
medieval. Includes pedigree of Somerville,
12-14th c.

Lincolnshire

Burwell

GOULDING, R.W. 'Notes on the lords of the
manor of Burwell', *A.A.S.R.P.* **24**(1), 1897,
62-94. Descent of manor, 11-19th c., through
Haye, Kyme, Cromwell, Brandon, Glemham
and Lister.

Driby

MASSINGBERD, W.O. 'Lords of the manor of
Driby', *A.A.S.R.P.* **23**(1), 1895, 106-34.
Includes many extracts from deeds, inquisition post mortems, etc., concerning the
families of Driby, Bernak, and Cromwell;
medieval.

Waddingworth

FLETCHER, W.G. DIMOCK. 'The manor of
Waddingworth, Co. Lincoln', *Reliquary* **15**
1874-5, 72. Descent of manor, 16-18th c.,
through Goodrich, Townshend, Dymocke and
Southwell.

Northamptonshire

Drayton House

SACKVILLE, S.G. STOPFORD. 'Drayton House',
A.A.S.R.P. **32**(1), 1913, 165-78. Includes
descent through De Vere, Drayton, Green,
Mordaunt, Germain, and Sackville.

Oxfordshire

Broughton Castle

SLADE, H. GORDON. 'Broughton Castle,
Oxfordshire', *A.J.* **135**, 1978, 138-94.
Includes pedigree showing descent of
Broughton through Wykeham, Fiennes and
Twisleton, 14-19th c., also pedigrees of
Broughton, 13-14th c., and Danvers and
Fermor, 16th c.

Rutland

Oakham

HARTSHORNE, CHARLES HENRY. 'The hall
of Oakham', *A.J.* **5**, 1845, 142-42. Rutland;
includes notes on the medieval descent of
the manor; with notices of Ferrers,
Mortimer, Bohun, etc.

Westmorland

Levens Hall

WESTON, G. F. 'Levens Hall, Westmoreland',
A.J. **26**, 1869, 97-120. Descent through
Levins, Bellingham and Grahme.

Worcestershire

Wanswell Court

COOKE, JAMES HERBERT. 'Wanswell Court
and its occupants for seven centuries',
A.A.S.R.P. **17**(1), 1883, 105-12. Wanswell,
Thorpe, Stone and Lysons families.

Yorkshire

Sheffield

TUCKER, STEPHEN I. 'Descent of the manor of Sheffield', *J.B.A.A.* **30**, 1874, 237-77. See 489-93 for an index. Includes schedules of taxpayers for the poll taxes of 1379 and 1692, and the hearth tax, 1665; also list of smiths and cutlers, 1670.

9. GENERAL HISTORICAL SOURCES, INCLUDING RECORDS OF ESTATE ADMINISTRATION

The articles listed here provide either lists of general sources for specific places, or abstracts of deeds, accounts, and other records of estate administration. Articles abstracting no more than two or three deeds have been excluded — a listing would take up more space than their genealogical value is worth. For most manorial records, see section 8. The records of ecclesiastical estate administration are dealt with in section 10.

A. GENERAL

MOORE, A. PERCIVAL. 'Marriage contracts or espousals in the reign of Queen Elizabeth I', *A.A.S.R.P.* **30**, 1909, 261-98.

B. BY PLACE

Berkshire

Hardwick

See Derbyshire. Chatsworth

Buckinghamshire

BIRCH, W. DE GRAY. 'Original documents in the possession of T. F. Halsey, esq., M.P.' *J.B.A.A.* **34**, 1884, 391-6. Medieval deeds, mainly relating to Buckinghamshire, especially Edlesburgh.

Caernarvonshire

Conway

FARRINGTON, T.B. 'Report on searches made at the Public Record Office in respect of the town of Conway or Aberconway', *J.B.A.A.* N.S., **4**, 1898, 201-22. Lists sources.

Derbyshire

FLETCHER, W.G. DIMOCK. 'Notes on Derbyshire ms. in the Bodleian Library at Oxford', *Reliquary* **23**, 1882-3, 160-62. List of mss.

JACKSON, CHARLES. 'Extracts from ancient deeds relating to Derbyshire in the possession of Charles Thorold, esq., of Welham, near Retford, Notts', *Reliquary* **20**, 1879-80, 109-12, 164-8 & 218-22. Medieval deeds.

SLEIGH, JOHN. 'An attempt at a Derbyshire glossary', *Reliquary* **5**, 1864-5, 156-64; **6**, 1865-6, 92-6 & 157-71.

Chatsworth

STALLYBRASS, BASIL. 'Bess of Hardwick's buildings and building accounts', *Arch.* **64**, 1913, 347-98. Includes list of craftsmen employed at Chatsworth, Derbyshire, and Hardwick, Berkshire, 16th c.

Wigwell Grange

JEWITT, LLEWELLYN. 'Wigwell Grange, in the county of Derby, and its connection with Darley Abbey', *Reliquary* **17**, 1876-7, 65-74, 161-8 & 225-34; **18**, 1877-8, 82-7 & 129-35. Medieval deeds.

Dorset

Sherborne

LEACH, ARTHUR F. 'Sherborne School before, under, and after Edward VI', *A.J.* **55**, 1898, 1-81. Includes rentals and accounts etc., giving names of tenants, etc.

Glamorganshire

C., G. T. 'An extent or survey by inquisition of the county of Glamorgan', *J.B.A.A.* **28**, 1871, 60-65. 13th c. knights' fees.

Gloucestershire

BIRCH, W. DE GREY. 'Original documents relating to Bristol and the neighbourhood', *J.B.A.A.* **31**, 1875, 289-305. See 516-8 for index. Includes medieval deeds, rental of 1445, etc.

'Gloucestershire charters' *A.J.* **29** 1872, 268-72. See also **28**, 1871, 159-60.

Kent

KERSHAW, S. W. 'Kent in the Lambeth archives', *J.B.A.A.* N.S. **3**, 1897, 185-91. Lists sources.

Leicestershire

FLETCHER, W.G.D. 'Some unpublished

documents relating to Leicestershire preserved in the Public Record Office', *A.A.S.R.P.* **23**(1), 1895, 213-52; **23**(2), 1896, 392-436; **24**(1), 1897, 234-77. Includes feet of fines and other deeds, chantry certificates, assize rolls, inquisitions post mortem, rentals, surveys, royalist composition papers, etc., including some documents now in the British Library.

THOMPSON, A. HAMILTON. 'Leicestershire documents, temp King John', *A.A.S.R.P.* **34**(1), 1917, 153-200. Feet of fines and extracts from Curia Regis rolls.

Noseley
HARTOPP, H. 'Some unpublished documents relating to Noseley, Co. Leicester', *A.A.S.R.P.* **25**(2), 1900, 431-58; **26**(1), 1901, 276-320. Deeds, etc., medieval.

Lincolnshire
BOYD, W. 'Calendar of all enrolments on the Close Rolls, temp. Henry VII, relating to the county of Lincoln', *A.A.S.R.P.* **23**(2), 1896, 260-73.

COLE, R.E.G. 'Observations on Gervase Holles' Lincolnshire notes, A.D. 1634-1642', *A.A.S.R.P.* **31**(2), 1912, 378-420. Intended as an introduction to vol 1 of the Lincoln Record Society; includes notes on some inscriptions, etc.

TURNER, EDMUND. 'Extracts from the household-book of Thomas Gray of Bassingthorpe, c. Lincoln', *Arch.* **11**, 1794, 22-33. Includes rental of 1577, of lands in Lincolnshire and Rutland, naming bailiffs.

Bourne
VENABLES, EDMUND. 'Bourne: its castle and its abbey', *A.A.S.R.P.* **20**(1), 1889, 1-19. Includes extracts from 16th c. accounts, giving some names; also a few deeds, etc.

Nocton
NORGATE, KATE, & FOOTMAN, MAURICE HENRY. 'Some notes for a history of Nocton', *A.A.S.R.P.,* **24**(2), 1897, 347-81. Includes pedigrees showing descent of manor from Darcy to Lymbury, Wymbishe, Towneley, Stanhope, Ellys, Bourke, and Robinson; also lists of vicars and priors, and extracts from the parish registers.

Norfolk
RYE, WALTER. 'The unpublished material for a history of the county of Norfolk', *A.J.* **47**, 1870, 164-9.

Oxfordshire
Great Milton
HARVEY, JOHN H. 'Great Milton, Oxfordshire and Thorncroft, Surrey: the building accounts for two manor-houses of the late fifteenth century', *J.B.A.A.* 3rd series, **18**, 1955, 42-56. Includes many names.

Rutland
See Lincolnshire.

Staffordshire
BIRCH, W. DE G. 'On documents in the possession of Lord Wrottesley of Wrottesley Hall, Staffordshire', *J.B.A.A.* **29**, 1873, 354-71. Staffordshire medieval deeds.

Suffolk
LEVIEN, EDWARD. 'On ms. collections relating to Suffolk in the British Museum', *J.B.A.A.* **21**, 1865, 5-21. Includes notes on many items of genealogical interest, including a volume of wills and deeds.

Surrey

Thorncroft
See Oxfordshire. Great Milton.

Sussex

Hastings
PRICE, E. B. 'Notes illustrative of some ancient deeds connected with the town of Hastings', *J.B.A.A.* **2**, 1847, 175-83. Includes deeds, plus the will of Richard Meihynge, 1436.

Yorkshire
ATKINSON, J.C. 'Some notes on personal names obtaining in Cleveland in 1302', *Reliquary* N.S. **4**, 1890, 201-7.

ATKINSON, J.C. 'Further remarks on personal names and their distribution in 1302', *Reliquary* N.S. **5**, 1891, 84-9. In North Riding, Yorkshire.

BAIN, JOSEPH. 'Notes on a collection of eight early documents relating to Yorkshire ...', *A.J.* **36**, 1879, 272-6. Miscellaneous medieval deeds.

WENTWORTH, GEORGE. 'Deeds relating to property in various parts of Yorkshire, from the muniment room at Woolley Park, near Wakefield', *A.J.* **18**, 1861, 60-65.

Murgatroyd
R., C.A. 'Murgatroyd evidences', *N.G.* **6**, 1903, 39-41. Deeds, 16-17th c.

C. BY FAMILY

Bertie
CLARK, G. T. 'Original documents of the Berties of Bertiestead or Bersted', *A.J.* **31**, 1874, 286-8. Kent deeds, medieval, with notes on the descent of Bertie.

Burgh
PERCEVAL, CHARLES SPENCER. 'Notes on a selection of ancient charters, letters, and other documents from the muniment-room of Sir John Lawson of Brough Hall, near Catterick, in Richmondshire, Baronet', *Arch.* **47**, 1883, 179-204. Title deeds etc. of Burgh family, medieval.

Clare
GUISEPPI, M.S. 'The wardrobe and household account of Bogo de Clare, A. D. 1284-6', *Arch.* **70**, 1920, 1-56. Includes many names.

Curzon
'Original documents: selections from the muniments of Lord Scarsdale', *A.J.* **29**, 1872, 83-90. Includes medieval pedigree of Curzon.

Giffard
'Charters relating to the family of Giffard', *J.B.A.A.* **8**, 1853, 347-51. Chillington, Sussex; medieval.

Gresley
HARLAND, JOHN. 'Chartulary of the Gresleys of Derbyshire', *Reliquary* **5**, 1864-5, 29-37; **6**, 1865-6, 79-86 & 139-47. Includes pedigrees and extracts from deeds.

Hyndlee
'Original documents: indenture of apprenticeship, temp. Ric II', *A.J.* **29**, 1872, 184-5. Between John Hyndlee of Northampton and Thomas Edward of Windsor.

Lathom
'Family of Lathom', *J.B.A.A.* **7**, 1851, 415-70. Cheshire; medieval deeds.

Lestrange
GURNEY, DAVID. 'Extracts from the household and privy purse accounts of the Lestranges of Hunstanton, from A.D.1519 to A.D.1578', *Arch.* **25**, 1834, 411-569. Includes many names.

Polsted
EVANS, JOHN. 'An account of the presents received and expenses incurred at the wedding of Richard Polsted of Albury, esquire, and Elizabeth, eldest daughter of William More of Loseley, esquire', *Arch.* **36**(1), 1855, 33-52. Albury, Hertfordshire and Loseley, Surrey. Includes many names.

Salven
GIBBONS, ALFRED. 'Salven v. Milles: an old matrimonial dispute', *N.G.* **6**, 1903, 74-80. Yorkshire; 1534 depositions.

Shareshull
'Sir William de Shareshull, Knight: a letter of consolation sent by Archbishop Alexander Nevile to him, on his entering the Order of Friars, c. 1375', *N.G.* **1**, 1895, 121.

Stafford
MARKLAND, JAMES HEYWOOD. 'Some remarks on the rent-roll of Humphrey, Duke of Buckingham', *A.J.* **8**, 1851, 259-81. Stafford family, 1447-8. Various counties.

Swynford
JARVIS, EDWIN GEORGE. 'Documents relating to the family of Swynford, from the Kettlethorpe title-deeds of Colonel Cracroft-Amcotts', *A.J.* **21**, 1864, 254-9. Lincolnshire; medieval deeds.

Sydney
KINGSFORD, C.L. 'On some ancient deeds and seals belonging to Lord de L'Isle and Dudley', *Arch.* **65**, 1914, 251-68. Medieval; includes brief notes on Sydney family.

10. ECCLESIASTICAL RECORDS

The articles listed in this section include many lists of clergymen, deed abstracts, records of ecclesiastical estate administration, etc. They do not, however, include churchwardens' accounts; for these, see below, section 11.

PALMER, C.F.R. 'Fasti ordinis fratrum praedicatorum: the provincials of the friar-preachers and black friars of England', *A.J.* **35**, 1878, 134-65.

Bedfordshire

BLAYDES, G.A. 'List of popish recusants for Bedfordshire: Mus. Brit., Add. Mss., 5494', *A.A.S.R.P.* **19**(1), 1887, 167-97. c.1642-8. *See also* Huntingdonshire. Ramsey

Bedford
WARMOLL, PROVOST. 'The Grey Friars Priory, Bedford', *A.A.S.R.P.* **16**(2), 1882, 265-73. Notes many names connected with the Priory.

Berkshire

Reading
WAY, ALBERT. 'Original documents, being contributions towards the history of Reading Abbey', *A.J.* **20**, 1863, 281-96; **22**, 1865, 151-61. Deeds, etc.

Cambridgeshire
'Diocesan registers, Ely', *N.G.* **2**, 1896, 17. Brief calendar of documents.

Carmarthenshire

St. Clears
See Devon, Barnstaple.

Cornwall

Truro
PALMER, C.F.R. 'The friar-preachers, or blackfriars, of Truro', *Reliquary* N.S. **2**, 1887, 11-15. Includes obits of religious, benefactors, etc.

Derbyshire
'Recusants in Derbyshire, 1577', *Reliquary* N.S. **7**, 1893, 116-7. List.

Ashford
'Original documents', *Reliquary* **2**, 1861-2,

97-8. Seating plan for the church at Ashford, Derbyshire, 1632.

Beauchief
KIRKE, HENRY. 'The Proemonstratensian abbey of Beauchief, in the county of Derby', *Reliquary* **7**, 1866-7, 193-206. Includes list of abbots, and many obits, with pedigree of Alfreton, 12-13th c.

Dale Abbey
FOX, SAMUEL. 'Dale Abbey, Derbyshire', *Reliquary* **8**, 1867-8, 193-206. Includes names of many associated with the Abbey at the Dissolution.

Dronfield
'Rectors and vicars of Dronfield', *Reliquary* **15**, 1874-5, 52.

Repton
ASHPITEL, A. 'On Repton church and priory', *J.B.A.A.* **7**, 1952, 263-83. Includes list of pensions paid and debts owing at the dissolution.

Devon

Barnstaple
GRAHAM, ROSE. 'The Cluniac priory of Saint-Martin des Champs, Paris, and its dependent priories in England and Wales', *J.B.A.A.* 3rd series, **11**, 1948, 35-39. Includes lists of priors at Barnstaple, St. James's by Exeter, and St. Clears, Carmarthenshire.

Buckland
See Plympton.

Canonsleigh
PERCEVAL, CHARLES SPENCER. 'Remarks on some early charters and documents relating to the Priory of Austin canons and Abbey of Austin canonesses at Canonsleigh in the county of Devon', *Arch.* **40**(2), 1866, 417-50. Includes medieval pedigrees of Claville, Beare, Arundel and Thorne.

Exeter
OLIVER, GEORGE. 'Ancient church within the Castle of Exeter', *A.J.* **11**, 1854, 157-64. Includes list of prebendaries of Hayes, Cutton, Carswell and Ashclist. *See also* Barnstaple

Plympton
'Original documents', *A.J.* **5**, 1848,

57-62. Medieval deeds of Plympton Priory and Buckland Abbey, Devon.

Essex
See also Huntingdonshire. Ramsey

Chelmsford
PALMER, C.F.R. 'The friar preachers, or blackfriars, of Chelmsford', *Reliquary* N.S. 3, 1889, 141-4. Includes notes on benefactors.

Thaxted
SYMONDS, GEORGE E. 'Thaxted and its cutlers' guild', *Reliquary* 5, 1864-5, 65-72. Includes list of vicars.

Gloucestershire

Bristol
ATCHLEY, E.G.C.F. 'Documents relating to the parish church of All Saints, Bristol', *A.J.* 58, 1901, 147-81. Various deeds and documents, including the will of Alice Halye, 1261.
NICHOLS, J.F. 'Old deeds of All Hallow Church, Bristol', *J.B.A.A.* 31, 1875, 259-65.
PALMER, C.F.R. 'The friar-preachers, or blackfriars, of Bristol', *Reliquary* N.S. 2, 1888, 71-83. Includes extracts from a martyrology, giving obits.

Cirencester
See Winchcombe.

Hayles
See Winchcombe.

Winchcombe
WALCOTT, MACKENZIE E. C. 'The abbeys of Winchcombe, Hayles, Cirencester, and Hales Owen', *J.B.A.A.* 34, 1878, 333-47. Winchcombe, Cirencester, and Hailes, Gloucestershire; Halesowen, Worcestershire; includes lists of abbots.

Hampshire

Andwell
GUNNER, W. H. 'An account of the alien priory of Andwell, or Enedewell, in Hampshire, a cell of the Abbey of Tyrone, with some remarks on the family of De Port of Basing, its founders', *A.J.* 9, 1852, 246-61. Includes pedigree of Port, 12-13th c.

Hamble
KIRBY, THOMAS F. 'The alien priory of St.

Andrew, Hamble, and its transfer to Winchester College in 1391', *Arch.* 50(2), 251-2. Includes list of 14th c. priors and deeds.

Winchester
PALMER, C.F.R. 'The friar-preachers, or blackfriars, of Winchester', *Reliquary* N.S. 3, 1889, 207-15. Includes notes on religious and benefactors.

Wyke
BAIGENT, FRANCES JOSEPH. 'On the parish church of Wyke, near Winchester', *J.B.A.A.* 19, 1863, 184-212. Includes list of rectors, with wills of William Atkinson, 1539, Nicholas Harpsfield, 1550, Agnes Complyn, 1553, and Stephen Complyn, 1543.

Herefordshire

Dilwyn
HEATHER, W. 'On Dilwyn Church', *J.B.A.A.* 27, 1871, 149-56. Includes list of vicars.

Wigmore
BRAKSPEAR, SIR HAROLD. 'Wigmore Abbey', *A.J.* 90, 1933, 26-51. Includes list of priors, and notes on the Mortimer family.

Huntingdonshire

Little Gidding
NOBLE, W. MACKRETH. 'Little Gidding and the Knights Templar', *J.B.A.A.* N.S. 6, 1900, 47-53. Includes list of rectors and patrons, 1226-1874.

Ramsey
BIRCH, W. DE G. 'Historical notes on the manuscripts belonging to Ramsey Abbey', *J.B.A.A.* N.S. 5, 1899, 229-42. Includes list of rolls, deeds, etc., for properties in Huntingdonshire and many other counties, but principally Bedfordshire, Cambridgeshire, Essex, Lincolnshire, Norfolk and Northamptonshire.

Kent

Canterbury
CROSS, FRANCIS W. 'The early minute books of the Dean and Chapter of Canterbury', *A.J.* 53, 1896, 235-48. 16-17th c.

Greenwich
MARTIN, A. R. 'The grey friars of

Greenwich', *A.J.* **80**, 1923, 81-114. Includes extracts from wills relating to the friars, 1482-1534.

Lancashire
'Confessions of a Lancashire priest, 1519', *N.G.* **2**, 1896, 128-30. Richard Thornton.

Furness
DELISLE, M. LEOPOLD. 'Documents relative to the Abbey of Furness, extracted from the archives of the Abbey of Savigny', *J.B.A.A.* **6**, 1851, 419-24. Medieval deeds.

Whalley
BIRCH, W. DE GRAY. 'Historical notes of Whalley Abbey', *J.B.A.A.* N.S. **1**, 1895, 161-6. Lists potential sources for the abbey's history, which may also yield genealogical information.

Leicestershire
FLETCHER, W.G.D. 'Documents relating to Leicestershire preserved in the episcopal registers at Lincoln', *A.A.S.R.P.* **21**(2), 1892, 277-329; **22**(1), 1893, 109-50; **22**(2), 1894, 227-365. Includes calendar of bishops registers, 13-18th c., brief list of 16th c. wills; list of incumbents, 1605, replies to visitation queries, early 18th c. (giving many names), etc, etc.
FOSTER, C.W. 'Admissions to benefices and compositions for first fruits in the county of Leicester, 1535-1660', *A.A.S.R.P.* **37**(1), 1925, 144-76; **37**(2), 1925, 322-36.
MOORE, A.P. 'Leicestershire livings in the reign of James I', *A.A.S.R.P.* **29**(1), 1908, 129-82. Includes lists, giving names of incumbents, etc.
MOORE, A. PERCIVAL. 'The metropolitical visitation of Archbishop Laud, with an appendix containing transcripts of documents in ecclesiastical suits of the period and other papers', *A.A.S.R.P.* **29**(2), 1908, 479-534. Lists clergy, 1634.
MOORE, A.P. 'Proceedings of the ecclesiastical courts in the Archdeaconry of Leicester', *A.A.S.R.P.* **28**(1), 1905, 117-220 & **28**(2), 1906, 593-662.
PEACOCK, EDWARD. 'Extracts from Lincoln episcopal visitations in the 15th, 16th and 17th centuries', *Arch.* **48**, 1835, 249-69. Includes lists of religious at Grace Dieu, Ouston, Launde and Leicester, with a number of legal cases concerning marriage, etc.

Gilmorton
BLOXSAM, MARTIN. 'The rectors of Gilmorton, including some notes on the parish', *A.A.S.R.P.* **30**(2), 1910, 391-462. List with biographical notes.

Leicester
THOMPSON, A. HAMILTON. 'The history of the hospital and new college of the Annunciation of Our Lady in the Newarke, Leicester', *A.A.S.R.P.* **32**(1), 1913, 245-92; **32**(2), 1914, 515-68; **33**(1), 1915, 178-215; **33**(2), 1916, 413-72. Includes lists of deans, canons and prebendaries.

Lincolnshire
FOSTER, C.W. 'Admissions to benefices in the Diocese of Lincoln, A.D. 1587-1660, as recorded in the bishops' certificates returned to the barons of the Exchequer', *A.A.S.R.P.* **30**(1), 1909, 47-118 & 379-90. See also 39, 1929, 179-216.
FOSTER, C.W. 'Institutions to benefices in the Diocese of Lincoln, 1540-1570. Calendar no.1', *A.A.S.R.P.* **24**(1), 1897, 1-32; **24**(2), 1898, 467-525. Includes index.
FOSTER, C.W. 'Institutions to benefices in the diocese of Lincoln, 1547-70, calendar no. II', *A.A.S.R.P.* **25**(2), 1900, 459-544. Includes index.
FOSTER, C.W. 'Certificate or return of all fees, annuities, corrodies, or pensions, payable to religious persons, 1555-6', *A.A.S.R.P.* **37**(2), 1925, 276-94.
FOSTER, C.W. 'Institutions to benefices in the Diocese of Lincoln', *A.A.S.R.P.* **39**, 1929, 179-216. 13th c., also includes supplement to 17th c. admissions (see above)
MADDISON, A.R. 'The transcripts in the Bishop of Lincoln's registry', **16**(2), 1882, 159-66. General description of the Diocesan archives.
THOMPSON, A. HAMILTON. 'Lambeth institutions to benefices: being a calendar of institutions to benefices in the old Diocese of Lincoln during vacancies of the episcopal see and during the visitations of the Diocese by the Archbishops of Canterbury as metropolitans, with collations of benefices made by the Archbishops jure devoluto, from the archiepiscopal registers in the library of Lambeth Palace, 1279-1532', *A.A.S.R.P.* **40**, 1930, 33-110.

THOMPSON, A. HAMILTON. 'Pluralism in the medieval church, with notes on pluralists in the Diocese of Lincoln, 1366', *A.A.S.R.P.* 33(1), 1915, 35-73; 34(1), 1917, 1-26; 35(1), 1918, 87-108; 35(2), 1920, 199-242; 36(1), 1921, 1-41.
VENABLES, PRECENTOR. 'The primary visitation of the Diocese of Lincoln by Bishop Neile, A.D. 1614', *A.A.S.R.P.* 16(1), 1881, 31-54. Includes list of ordinands, 1617-19, and names of 'lecturers', i.e., preachers, in the diocese.
WORDSWORTH, CHR. 'Lincolnshire charities', *N.G.* 1, 1895, 152-5. Brief note on a survey.
'Some notes of Roman Catholics in Lincolnshire', *N.G.* 2, 1896, 208; 3, 1900, 102-4. Gives parishes, but few surnames, 1604-5 and 1780, from clergy returns.
See also Huntingdonshire, Ramsey

Bardney
BRAKSPEAR, HAROLD. 'Bardney Abbey', *A.J.* 79, 1922, 1-92. Includes many monumental inscriptions, 13-16th c., with survey, 16th c., giving names of tenants.

Carlton Hundred
DUDDING, R.C. 'The East Lindsey Carltons', *A.A.S.R.P.* 39, 1929, 264-72; 40, 1930, 15-29. Carlton Hundred and the manors of Castle, Great and Little Carlton; includes lists of early incumbents and patrons.

Gokewell
LOWE, F. PYNDAR. 'On some charters relating to the nunnery of Gokewell in Lincolnshire', *A.A.S.R.P.* 3(1), 1854, 102-8. 12th c.

Graffoe Deanery
COLE, R.E.G. 'Notes on the ecclesiastical history of the Deanery of Graffoe to the close of the fourteenth century', *A.A.S.R.P.* 24(2), 1898, 381-448. Includes list of institutions to benefices, 1209-1405.
COLE, R.E.G. 'Notes on the ecclesiastical history of the Deanery of Graffoe during the fifteenth and sixteenth centuries', 25(1), 1899, 47-120; 25(2), 1900, 253-309. Includes institutions to benefices, 1405-1705, etc.
COLE, R.E.G. 'Notes on the ecclesiastical history of Graffoe during the eighteenth and nineteenth centuries', *A.A.S.R.P.* 26(1), 1901, 97-163. Includes institutions, 1705-1901.

Kettlethorpe
COLE, R.E.G. 'The manor and rectory of Kettlethorpe in the parts of Lindsey in the county of Lincoln', *A.A.S.R.P.* 31(1), 1911, 41-86. Includes list of rectors and pedigree of Swynford, 14-16th c., etc.

Lincoln
MADDISON, A.R. 'Lincoln Cathedral choir, A.D. 1558 to 1640', *A.A.S.R.P.* 18(1), 1885, 110-22. Gives names of many vicars choral, with abstracts of the wills of Thomas Floure, 1555; William Freman, 1558, Robert Hurstcrafte, 1611 and George Huddleston, 1611.
MADDISON, A.R. 'Lincoln Cathedral choir, A.D. 1700-1750', *A.A.S.R.P.* 20(2), 1890, 213-26. Includes names of vicars and choristers.
MADDISON, A.R. 'Lincoln Cathedral choir, A.D. 1750-1875', *A.A.S.R.P.* 21(2), 1892, 208-26. Gives names of vicars choral; also includes a few monumental inscriptions.
MASSINGBERD, W.O. 'Lincoln Cathedral charters', *A.A.S.R.P.* 26(1), 1901, 18-96; 26(2), 1902, 321-69; 27(1), 1903, 1-91. Medieval.
VENABLES, PRECENTOR. 'Bishop Antony Beeke's register of the Prebendaries of Lincoln, 1333, and 1343', *A.J.* 42, 1885, 469-75.
WICKENDEN, PREB. 'Contents of the muniment room of Lincoln Cathedral', *A.J.* 28, 1881, 309-15.
WORDSWORTH, PREB. 'The names of the companie of ringers of our Blessed Virgen Marie of Lincolne', *A.A.S.R.P.* 20(2), 1890, 241-3. 1614-1725.

Moulton
FOSTER, W.E. 'On the history of All Saints Church, Moulton', *A.A.S.R.P.* 20(2), 1890, 249-63. Includes list of vicars, etc.

Norton Disney
'Institutions of Norton Disney, Co. Lincoln', *N.G.* 1, 1895, 108-9.

Sempringham
FOSTER, C.W. 'Grants to Sempringham Priory by members of the Langton family', *A.A.S.R.P.* 37(2), 1925, 241-6. Deeds with 12-13th c. pedigree.

London and Middlesex

Friars Minors
SHEPHERD, E. B. S. 'The church of the Friars Minors in London', *A.J.* 59, 1902, 238-87. Includes extensive list of burials.

St. Bartholomew, West Smithfield
WEBB, E. B. 'Notes on the Augustinian Priory

of St. Bartholomew, West Smithfield', *Arch.* 59, 1905, 375-90. Includes lists of priors, 1123-1559, and rectors, 1539-1887.

St. Helens
MALCOLM, J. P. 'A survey of the Priory of St. Helen's in London, taken in the twenty-third year of King Henry the Eighth', *Arch.* 16, 1809, 29-31.

Westminster Abbey
BURTT, JOSEPH. 'Some account of the muniments of the Abbey of Westminster', *A.J.* 29, 1872, 135-50.

Norfolk
See also Huntingdonshire. Ramsey

Great Yarmouth
PALMER, C.F.R. 'The friar-preachers, or blackfriars, of Great Yarmouth, Norfolk', *Reliquary* N.S. 1, 1897, 139-46. Includes obits of religious, benefactors, etc.

Kings Lynn
PALMER, C.F.R. 'The friar-preachers, or black friars of Kings Lynn', *A.J.* 41, 1884, 79-86. Includes lists of benefactors, and notes on individual friars.

Norwich
PALMER, C.F.R. 'The friar-preachers, or blackfriars of Norwich', *Reliquary* N.S. 2, 1888, 161-70 & 210-14; 3, 1889, 42-9 & 98-103. Includes names of priors, notes on benefactors, obits, etc.

Thetford
PALMER, C.F.R. 'The friar-preachers, or blackfriars, of Thetford', *Reliquary* N.S. 1, 1887, 196-204. Includes obits of religious, benefactors, etc.

Northamptonshire
HILL, J.H. 'The Bishopric of Peterborough, and its prelates', *A.A.S.R.P.* 10(2), 1870, 313-30. Includes list of bishops, with biographical notes.
LONGDEN, H. ISHAM. 'Early Northamptonshire clergy', *A.A.S.R.P.* 42(1), 1936, 145-51.
SERJEANTSON, R.M. 'Sanctuary seekers in Northamptonshire'. *A.A.S.R.P.* 32(1), 1913, 179-228; 32(2), 1914, 423-84. Includes many names of medieval criminals.
See also Huntingdonshire. Ramsey

Fotheringhay
COX, J.C. 'The College of Fotheringhay', *A.J.* 61, 1904, 241-75. Includes full transcript of the college sacrist's accounts, 1540-41, giving names of parishioners who made offerings, etc.

Irthlingborough
THOMPSON, A. HAMILTON. 'Early history of the College of Irthlingborough', *A.A.S.R.P.* 35(1), 1918, 267-92. Includes list of deans and canons.

Kingsthorpe
MARKHAM, CHRISTOPHER A. 'The hospital of Saint David, or the Holy Trinity, Kingsthorp, Northamptonshire', *A.A.S.R.P.* 24(1), 1897, 164-74. Includes list of masters.

Peterborough
WALCOTT, MACKENZIE E.C. 'Notes on Peterborough Cathedral, with a list of the abbots of Leicester appended', *A.A.S.R.P.* 14, 1878, 272-7.

Nottinghamshire

Blyth
VENABLES, EDMUND. 'The Benedictine Priory of the Blessed Virgin Mary, Blyth, Nottinghamshire', *A.A.S.R.P.* 15(2), 1880, 141-67. Includes list of priors, etc.

Newstead
GRESLEY, JOHN MOREWOOD. 'The Austin Priory of St. Mary of Newstead in Shirwood, Nottinghamshire', *Reliquary* 1, 1860-61, 197-205. Includes list of priors.

Nottingham Archdeaconry
'Registry of the Archdeaconry of Nottingham', *N.G.* 1, 1895, 168. Brief calendar of documents.

Worksop
STACYE, J. 'The Priory and parish church of Worksop or Radford, Nottinghamshire', *J.B.A.A.* 30, 1874, 156-74. Includes much genealogical information on Lovetot, Furnival and Nevil families.

Oxfordshire
Witney
NORRIS, W. FOXLEY. 'Memoranda relating to Witney, Oxon.' *J.B.A.A.* 47, 1891, 120-23. List of rectors, with brief biographical notes.

Shropshire

Bridgenorth
CLARK-MAXWELL, W. G., & THOMPSON, A. HAMILTON. 'The College of St. Mary Magdalene, Bridgenorth, with some account of the deans and prebendaries', *A.J.* **84**, 1927, 1-87. Includes lists of deans and canons, c.1161-1545, with biographical notes on the deans.

Staffordshire

Burton-on-Trent
BIRCH, W. 'Some new contributions towards the history of the Benedictine Abbey of Burton-on-Trent, Co. Stafford', *J.B.A.A.* N.S. **2**, 1896, 245-315. Lists abbots.

Suffolk

Butley
MYRES, J. N. L. 'Butley Priory, Suffolk', *A.J.* **90**, 1933, 177-281. Includes list of priors and canons, list of 26 wills mentioning the Priory, and detailed abstracts of the wills of William Pakeman 1504, and Henry Baret, 1516/7.

Ipswich
PALMER, C.F.R. 'The friar-preachers, or blackfriars, of Ipswich', *Reliquary* N.S. **1**, 1887, 70-78. Includes obits of religious, benefactors, etc.

Mettingham
MANNING, C. R. 'Extracts from the ancient accounts of Mettingham College, Suffolk', *A.J.* **6**, 1849, 62-8. Includes many 14th c. names.

Surrey

Bermondsey
GRAHAM, ROSE. 'Priory of Charite-sur-Loire and the monastery of Bermondsey', *J.B.A.A.* N.S. **32**, 1926, 157-91. Includes list of Bermondsey priors and abbots.

Chertsey
WAY, ALBERT. 'Notices of a register of the acts of John de Rutherwyke, Abbot of Chertsey in the reigns of Edward II and Edward III', *A.J.* **19**, 1862, 350-6.

Guildford
PALMER, C.F.R. 'The friar-preachers, or blackfriars, of Guildford', *Reliquary* N.S. **1**, 1887, 7-20. Includes obits of religious, benefactors, etc.

Wadhurst
'The church of St. Peter and Paul, Wadhurst, Surrey', *J.B.A.A.* **23**, 1867, 366-9. Includes list of vicars.

Sussex

Chichester
WALCOTT, MACKENZIE E. C. 'Fasti Cicestrenses, *J.B.A.A.* **22**, 1866, 110-56 & 463-8. Lists Chichester Cathedral clergy.

Lewes
SIMS, RICHARD. 'Account of the existing cartularies of religious houses in Sussex, particularly that of the Priory of Lewes', *J.B.A.A.* **42**, 1886, 355-78. Includes notes on Battle, Bayham and Sele families, with detailed abstract of Lewes chartulary.

Ringmer
LEGGE, W. HENEAGE. 'The church of Ringmer, Sussex', *Reliquary and the illustrated archaeologist*, N.S., **4**, 1898, 224-37. Includes list of incumbents.

Robertsbridge
PERCEVAL, CHARLES SPENCER. 'Remarks on some charters and other documents relating to the Abbey of Robertsbridge, in the county of Sussex ...', *Arch.* **45**, 1880, 427-61. Includes list of abbots.

Wiltshire

Malmesbury
BIRCH, W. DE G. 'On the succession of the abbots of Malmesbury', *J.B.A.A.* **27**, 1871, 314-42. List of abbots, with biographical notes; also includes notes on the Abbey's records.

Salisbury
EDWARDS, KATHLEEN. 'The houses of Salisbury Close in the fourteenth century', *J.B.A.A.* 3rd series **4**, 1939, 55-115. Includes extensive lists of clergy occupants of houses in the Close.

Worcestershire
CREIGHTON, CANON. 'The Italian bishop of Worcester', *A.A.S.R.P.* **20**(1), 1889, 94-118. Includes receiver-generals accounts, c.1534, giving many names.

NOAKE, J. 'Worcester Consistory Court', *Reliquary* N.S. **6**, 1892, 230-4. Includes list of offenders appearing before the court in July 1693.
WILLIS-BUND, J.W. 'Religious life in Worcestershire in the seventeenth century, shown by the sessions records', *A.A.S.R.P.* **24**(2), 1898, 574-96.
'Recusants in Worcestershire and Warwickshire, 1577', *Reliquary* N.S. **7**, 1893, 230-1. Lists.

Halesowen
See Gloucestershire. Winchcombe

Pershore
WALCOTT, MACKENZIE E. C. 'The Benedictine Abbey of St. Mary, Pershore', *J.B.A.A.* **32**, 1876, 330-43. Includes list of abbots.

Worcester
LEES, EDWIN. 'History of the Convent of the White Ladies, Worcester', *A.A.S.R.P.* **8**(2), 1866, 355-64. Includes list of prioresses.

Yorkshire
'Archiepiscopal visitations of the Dioceses of York and Chester', *N.G.* **2**, 1896, 76-8. List of surviving visitation books.
'Papist returns to the Archbishop of York in the 18th century', *N.G.* **3**, 1900, 4-8, 84-91 & 177-80; **4**, 1901, 34-6. Selected returns from throughout Yorkshire, but especially Aberford, Leeds, Everingham, York, the Ainsty and the North Riding.
'Presentments of Papist recusants, 1597: the presentments of vicars, parsons, and curates against recusants', *N.G.* **6**, 1903, 31-6. West Riding.

Beverley
ELLIS, HENRY. 'An account of the register of persons who sought sanctuary at St. John of Beverley in Yorkshire, preserved among the Harleian Manuscripts in the British Museum', *Arch.* **17**, 1814, 198-200. 15th c.

Bridlington
SOLLOWAY, J. 'The Austin canons of Bridlington', *A.A.S.R.P.* **33**(1), 1915, 142-60. Includes list of priors, etc.

Kirkstall
'Kirkstall Abbey', *N.G.* **2**, 1896, 118-9. List of benefactors.

Richmond Archdeaconry
'Diocesan registries: registry of Ripon (Archdeaconry of Richmond)', *N.G.* **1**, 1895, 167-8. Brief calendar of documents.

Rievaulx
COPPACK, GLYN. 'Some descriptions of Rievaulx Abbey in 1538-9: the disposition of a major Cistercian precinct in the early sixteenth century', *J.B.A.A.* **139**, 1986, 100-33. Includes survey giving names of tenants.

Wath
LUKIS, W.C. 'The church of Wath, near Ripon', *A.A.S.R.P.* **13**(1), 1875, 75-87. Includes list of rectors, with biographical notes; also notes on brasses, etc.

Yarm
PALMER, C.F.R. 'The friar-preachers or black friars of Yarm', *A.J.* **87**, 1880, 184-92. Includes biographical notes on some friars, list of burials, and notes on bequests to the Friary.

York
KERRY, CHAS. 'History and antiquities of All Saints Church, North Street, York', *A.A.S.R.P.* **9**(1), 1867, 57-69. Includes list of 18-19th c. rectors and medieval chantry chaplains, with notes on monuments, extracts from wills, etc.
SOLLOWAY, J. 'St. Mary's Abbey, York', *A.A.S.R.P.* **30**(1), 1909, 231-42. Includes list of abbots.

11. OFFICIAL LISTS OF NAMES AND OTHER RECORDS OF NATIONAL GOVERNMENT

DILLON, VISCOUNT. 'The rack', *A.J.* **62**, 1905, 48-66. With names of sufferers, 16th c.
PEACOCK, EDWARD. 'Names of the collectors of the Roman Catholic contribution for carrying on the war against the Scots, A.D. 1638', *Reliquary* **13**, 1872-3, 67-9. List covering all counties.
SIMPSON, JUSTIN. 'Gleanings from the Close Rolls of Henry III', *Reliquary* **26**, 1885-6,

145-9, 213-21 & 269-75; N.S., 1, 1887, 47-9 & 112-3; 3, 1889, 176-8.
STAPLETON, THOMAS. 'A brief summary of the wardrobe accounts of the 10th, 11th and 14th years of King Edward the Second', *Arch.* 26, 1836, 318-45. Includes many names; records a few births, marriages and deaths.
'Gentlemen knighted at Hutton Field in Scotland, 1482', *N.G.* 2, 1896, 83-4.
'A list of the lords spiritual and temporal, knights and esquires, whose names appear to be in the commissions of peace, and of oyer and terminer, on the 12th of November, 2nd Henry VII, 1487', *Reliquary* 25, 1884-5, 32. For Derbyshire, Nottinghamshire, Staffordshire and Yorkshire, West Riding.
'Notice of documents preserved in the Record Office at Malta', *A.J.* 7, 1850, 369-73.

Cumberland

'A Cumberland riot: Star Chamber proceedings, bundle 19, no. 7: riot at Brydekerke, temp. Henry VIII', *N.G.* 2, 1896, 37-8.

Derbyshire

'A list of gentlemen in Derbyshire and how they stand affected', *Reliquary* N.S. 6, 1892, 112-3. c.1663.

Derby

'Derby estreats, 17th Charles I, 1641', *Reliquary* 25, 1884-5, 26. Brief list of city tax payers.

Hope

DANIEL-TYSSEN, R. 'Contributions towards a history of the parish of Hope, in the county of Derby', *Reliquary* 11, 1870-71, 167-72 & 237-42; 12, 1871-2, 41-4. Includes lay subsidies, 1431, 1535, 1546, 1551, 1552, 1571, and 1576; also pedigrees of Eyre, medieval-17th c.

Marston Montgomery

'Original documents', *Reliquary* 2, 1861-2, 34-6. Late 17th c. lists of poll tax payers, for Marston Montgomery.

Wormhill

'Original documents', *Reliquary* 7, 1866-7, 184-5. Tax assessment, 1696, for Wormhill.

Co. Durham

'Knights of the Bishopric of Durham present at the Battle of Lewes, 1264', *N.G.* 4, 1901, 49-51.

Kent

Ruxley Hundred

MANDY, W. H. 'A Kentish hundred: pleas of the Crown for the hundred of Ruxley, with a running commentary', *J.B.A.A.* N.S. 22, 1916, 245-54. Assize roll, 1227; includes many names.

Lancashire

Claughton

FISHWICK, MAJOR. 'War tax for the township of Claughton in 1689', *Reliquary* 11, 1870-71, 79-80. List of those assessed for the 'aid' of 1689.

Leicestershire

FLETCHER, WILLIAM GEORGE DIMOCK. 'The earliest Leicestershire lay subsidy roll, 1327', *A.A.S.R.P.* 19(2), 1888, 209-312 & 447-8; 20(1), 1889, 131-78.
HARTOPP, HENRY. 'Leicestershire lay subsidy roll, 1603-4', *A.A.S.R.P.* 24(2), 1898, 601-27.
MOORE, A. PERCIVAL. 'Subsidies of the clergy in the Archdeaconry of Leicester in the 17th cent.' *A.A.S.R.P.* 27(2), 1904, 445-95. With names.

Lincolnshire

MADDISON, A.R. 'Lincolnshire gentry during the sixteenth century', *A.A.S.R.P.* 22(2), 1894, 174-222. Includes genealogical notes on those involved in the Lincolnshire rising of 1536; also list of those supplying lances and horse in the muster of 1586.
SIMPSON, JUSTIN. 'Lincolnshire contributors to the royal loan to Charles I, 1625', *Reliquary* 25, 1884-5, 14-16.
SWALES, T.H. 'The Parliamentary enclosures of Lindsey', *A.A.S.R.P.* 42(2), 1937, 233-74. Lincolnshire; includes list of proprietors for Anderby Outmarsh.
WATERS, E. CHESTER. 'Roll of landowners in Lindsey, temp. Henry I (Cotton Ms., Claudius, c.5)', *A.A.S.R.P.* 16(2), 1882, 166-230. Survey of landowners, c.1114-16, with many names.

London

STAHLSCHMIDT, J. C. L. 'Original documents', *A.J.* 44, 1887, 56-82. Lay subsidy return for the City of London, 1412.

Northamptonshire
DRYDEN, SIR H. 'The Northamptonshire militia in the reigns of King Henry VIII and Queen Elizabeth', *A.A.S.R.P.* **20**(2), 1890, 352-79. Includes many names of those mustered.
SIMPSON, JUSTIN. 'Northamptonshire contributors to the royal loan to Charles I, 1625', *Reliquary* **25**, 1883-4, 237-9. List.

Rutland
SIMPSON, JUSTIN. 'Rutlandshire contributors to the royal loan to Charles I, 1625', *Reliquary* **26**, 1885-6, 67-8. List.

Worcestershire
GREENSTREET, JAMES. 'List of inhabitants of Worcestershire in 28 Henry VI (A.D. 1449-50)', *Reliquary* N.S. **4**, 1890, 243-5. From the De Banco rolls.

Yorkshire
COX, J. CHARLES. 'Sanctuaries and sanctuary seekers of Yorkshire', *A.J.* **68**, 191, 273-299. 'The rebellion of 1745: accounts, correspondence, and muster rolls of the Yorkshire Association, in the possession of the Archbishop of York', *N.G.* **3**, 1900, 17-24. Includes many names.

Holderness
BLASHILL, THOMAS. 'Some certificates as to recusants in Holderness', *J.B.A.A.* N.S. **3**, 1897, 275-80.

12. COUNTY, MUNICIPAL AND PAROCHIAL ARCHIVES, INCLUDING CHURCHWARDEN'S ACCOUNTS, ETC

Many documents found in parish chests were published or discussed in the six journals under consideration, and these articles are listed here. Also included are a number of general parochial histories which include pedigrees, lists of monumental inscriptions, incumbents, wills, etc.

Bedfordshire

Luton
'Road cross at Luton, Bedfordshire', *N.G.* **2**, 1896, 70-71. Certificate with signatures of some parishioners, 1574.

Berkshire

Abington
WARD, J. 'Extracts from the church-wardens' accounts of the parish of St. Helen, in Abington, Berkshire, from the first year of the reign of Philip and Mary to the thirty-fourth year of Q. Elizabeth ...', *Arch.* **1**, 1770, 11-23.

Buckinghamshire

Wing
OUVRY, FREDERIC. 'Extracts from the churchwardens' accounts of the parish of Wing, in the county of Buckingham', *Arch.* **36**(2), 1856, 219-41. Includes names.
LLOYD, L. H. 'The Churchwardens' accounts of Wing, Co. Bucks', *J.B.A.A.* **44**, 1888, 51-9. 16th c.

Cheshire
BLACK, W.H. 'On the records of the County Palatine of Chester', *J.B.A.A.* **5**, 1850, 187-95.

Cornwall

Marazion
LACH-SZYRMA, W. S. 'Notes on the borough records of the towns of Marazion, Penzance, and St. Ives', *J.B.A.A.* **38**, 1882, 354-70.

Penzance
See Marazion.

St. Ives
See Marazion.

St. Neots
LEFROY, SIR J. H. 'Parochial accounts, seventeenth century, St. Neots, Cornwall', *A.J.* **48**, 1891, 65-76.

Stratton
PEACOCK, EDWARD. 'On the churchwardens' accounts of the parish of Stratton, in the county of Cornwall', *Arch.* **46**, 1881, 195-236. Transcripts, 16th c.

Derbyshire
'Petitions, grants and declarations concerning

Derbyshire miners, 1641-2', *Reliquary* **23**, 1882-3, 113-5. Includes names of 21 petitioners.

Derby
WALLIS, ALFRED. 'Exeter Bridge, Derby', *Reliquary* **13**, 1872-3, 203-5. Includes names of many petitioners, 1810, opposing the building of a bridge.

Holmesfield
JACKSON, CHARLES. 'Notes from the 'book of record' for the inhabitants of Holmesfield, Derbyshire', *Reliquary* **20**, 1879-80, 17-19. 16-18th c. notes on deaths and heirs of tenants, etc.

Morton
KERRY, CHARLES. 'Desultory notes on the old churchwardens' book of the parish of Morton, Co. Derby, 1592-1642', *Reliquary* **25**, 1884-5, 17-25.

Devon

Exeter
WRIGHT, T. 'The municipal archives of Exeter', *J.B.A.A.* **18**, 1862, 306-17.

Plymouth
WORTH, R. N. 'On the Plymouth municipal records', *J.B.A.A.* **39**, 1883, 110-8

Woodbury
ELLACOMBE, H.T. 'Malt rate levied in the parish of Woodbury, Co. Devon, from a ms. in the possession of the late General Lee of Efford Barton', *A.J.* **40**, 1883, 225-33. List of parishioners, 1536.

Dorset
HALLIWELL, J. D. 'On the municipal archives of Dorset', *J.B.A.A.* **28**, 1872, 28-31.

Essex

Colchester
BENHAM, W. BURNEY. 'The town charters and other borough records of Colchester, *A.J.* **64**, 1907, 203-9.

Gloucestershire

Minchinhampton
BRUCE, JOHN. 'Extracts from accounts of the churchwardens of Minchinhampton, in the county of Gloucester, with observations thereon', *Arch.* **35**, 1854, 409-52.

Hampshire

Portsmouth
SAUNDERS, W. H. 'Churchwardens' accounts of St. Thomas, Portsmouth, A.D. 1566', *J.B.A.A.* **44**, 1888, 257-63.

Southampton
VAUX, W. S. W. 'Some notices of records preserved amongst the Corporation archives at Southampton', *A.J.* **3**, 1846, 229-33.

Winchester
COLLIER, I.C. 'The churchwardens' accounts of St. John the Baptist, Winchester', *Reliquary* **17**, 1876-7, 81-5, 155-7 & 219-24. 16-17th c.
SMIRKE, E. 'Winchester in the thirteenth century', *A.J.* **7**, 1850, 372-83. Inquest giving names of jurors, and making reference to a list of tenants.

Hertfordshire

St. Albans
BLACK, W. H. 'On the town records of St. Albans', *J.B.A.A.* **26**, 1870, 143-9.

Kent

Canterbury
WRIGHT, THOMAS. 'On the municipal archives of the City of Canterbury', *Arch.* **31**, 1846, 198-211.

Dover
KNOCKER, EDWARD. 'The archives of the borough of Dover', *J.B.A.A.* **40**, 1884, 1-14.
SIMS, R. 'Dover records in the British Museum', *J.B.A.A.* **40**, 1884, 129-32.

Eltham
CORNER, G. R. 'Extracts from the churchwardens' accounts of the parish of Eltham in Kent', *Arch.* **34**, 1852, 51-65. Includes names.

Lancashire

Salford
MAKINSON, C. 'On the ancient court records of the Borough of Salford', *J.B.A.A.* N.S. **1**, 1895, 314-26. 17th c.

Leicestershire
FLETCHER, W.G.D. 'The Lords Lieutenant of Leicestershire', *A.A.S.R.P.* **26**(1), 1901, 259-71. Includes biographical notes.
FREER, W.J. 'Clerks of the Peace and

Lieutenancy for Co. Leicester', *A.A.S.R.P.* **26**(1), 1901, 272-6. Partial list; 1558-1888. 'Extracts from the Curia Regis rolls relating to Leicestershire, A.D. 1211-1269'. *A.A.S.R.P.* **34**(2), 1918, 363-413; **35**(1), 1920, 109-99; **35**(2), 1921, 305-22. Includes pedigrees of Botiller, Powtrel, Roppesley, Lekeburn and Turvill.

Appleby Magna
FALKNER, T.F. 'Churchwardens' accounts of Appleby Magna', *Reliquary* **13**, 1872-3, 111-4. Includes some names of churchwardens, etc., 17-18th c.

Ayleston
DARE, M.P. 'Old time lawkeepers: a study of the constables of Ayleston, Leics., and their accounts, 1671-1710', *A.A.S.R.P.* **38**, 1926, 106-65. Includes list of constables, with other names.

Leicester
THOMPSON, JAMES. 'The rolls of the mayors of Leicester', *A.A.S.R.P.* **12**(2), 1874, 261-74. Notes on medieval mayors.

Loughborough
'The churchwardens accounts of Loughborough', *Reliquary* **13**, 1872-3, 201-2. Includes a few names, 17th c.

Market Harborough
STOCKS, J.E. 'On ancient charters and other documents lately dicovered at Market Harborough, Leicestershire', *A.A.S.R.P.* **16**(2), 1882, 284-90. Brief discussion of 172 medieval documents found in the parish chest.

Melton Mowbray
NORTH, MR. 'The constables of Melton in the reign of Queen Elizabeth', *A.A.S.R.P.* **8**(1), 1865, 185-204. Includes extracts from accounts, with some names.

Stathern
GUILFORD, EVERARD L. 'Accounts of the constables of the village of Stathern, Leics', *A.J.* **69**, 1912, 125-60. 1630-49.

Lincolnshire

Conisholme
DUDDING, REGINALD C. 'Conisholme', *A.A.S.R.P.* **41**(2), 1935, 119-40. Includes pedigrees of Copley, 16th c., Tempest, Berkeley and Pakenham, 16-17th c., Dymock,

15-17th c., with list of early incumbents and patrons.

Grimsby
'Grimsby burgess roll, 29 Hen. VI - 44 Eliz', *N.G.* **1**, 1895, 1-4, 67-72, 140-41 & 225-6.

Leverton
PEACOCK, EDWARD. 'Extracts from the churchwardens' accounts of the parish of Leverton, in the county of Lincoln', *Arch.* **41**(2), 1867, 333-70.

Lincoln
HILL, J.W.F. 'Three lists of the mayors, bailiffs and sheriffs of Lincoln', *A.A.S.R.P.* **39**, 1929, 217-56.

Louth
BANKS, SIR JOSEPH. 'Extracts out of an old book relating to the building of Louth steeple, and repairing the church, &c., from about the year 1500 or 1501, to 1518', *Arch.* **10**, 1792, 70-98. Accounts, giving many names.

Potter Hanworth
NORGATE, KATE & FOOTMAN, M.H. 'Some notes for a history of Potter Hanworth', *A.A.S.R.P.* **26**(2), 1962, 369-93. Includes pedigree of D'Eyncourt, 11-14th c., list of rectors, a few deeds, etc.

Sutterton
PEACOCK, EDWARD. 'Churchwardens' accounts of St. Mary's, Sutterton', *A.J.* **39**, 1882, 53-63. 15-16th c.

London and Middlesex
WEAVER, L. 'The complete building accounts of the city chambers (parochial) designed by Sir Christopher Wren', *Arch.* **66**, 1914-15, 1-60. 17th c., includes lists of tradesmen.

St. Barthomolew by the Exchange
See St. Margaret-Lothbury.

St. Christopher-Le-Stocks
See St. Margaret-Lothbury.

St. Margaret-Lothbury
FRESHFIELD, EDWIN. 'On the parish books of St. Margaret-Lothbury, St. Christopher-Le-Stocks, and St. Bartholomew-by-the-Exchange, in the city of London', *Arch.* **45**(1), 1877, 57-123. 15-17th c.

St. Matthew, Friday Street
SIMPSON, W. SPARROW. 'Churchwardens' accounts for the parish of St. Matthew, Friday Street, in the city of London, from 1547 to 1603', *J.B.A.A.* **25**, 1869, 356-81.

St. Peter Cheap
SIMPSON, W. SPARROW. 'On the parish of St. Peter Cheap, in the city of London, from 1392 to 1633, *J.B.A.A.* **24**, 1868, 248-68. Extracts from the churchwarden's accounts.

St. Stephen, Coleman Street
FRESHFIELD, EDWIN. 'Some remarks upon the book of records and history of the parish of St. Stephen, Coleman Street, in the city of London, *Arch.* **50**(1), 1887, 17-87. 15th c.

Norfolk
Kings Lynn
GURNEY, HUDSON. 'Extracts from a manuscript containing portions of the proceedings of the corporation of Lynn Regis, in Norfolk from 1430 to 1731, taken from the hall books', *Arch.* **24**, 1932, 317-28. Includes many names of mayors, merchants, members of parliament, etc., mainly 15-16th c.

Northamptonshire
MARKHAM, C.A. 'The Lords Lieutenant and county officials of Northamptonshire', *A.A.S.R.P.* **26**(2), 1902, 415-41. List, with genealogical and biographical notes.

Rutland
Glaston
WORDSWORTH, CHR. 'Some parochial papers relating to Glaston, in the county of Rutland', *Reliquary* N.S. **4**, 1890, 236-40; **5**, 1891, 40-44 & 153-62. Settlement papers and overseers' accounts, etc.

Shropshire
Ludlow
WRIGHT, THOMAS. 'A few notes of the early churchwardens' accounts of the town of Ludlow', *J.B.A.A.* **23**, 1867, 309-26.

Shrewsbury
FLETCHER, W. G. D. 'The municipal records of Shrewsbury', *A.J.* **51**, 1894, 283-92.

Sussex
Ringmer
LEGGE, W. HENEAGE. 'The parish documents of Ringmer of the Jacobean and Georgian periods', *Reliquary and illustrated archaeologist*, N.S., **5**, 1899, 217-26.

Warwickshire
Coventry
HARRIS, M. D. 'Coventry leet book', *J.B.A.A.* N.S. **16**, 1910, 65-70.

Wiltshire
Wilton
'Wilton corporation charters', *J.B.A.A.* **17**, 1861, 311-18. Includes medieval deeds etc., with will of John Fromond, 1348.

Worcestershire
LEA, W., WALKER, J. SEVERN, & HOPKINS, W. JEFFREY. 'Notes on the churches of Hampton Lovett; S. Peter and S. Andrew, Droitwich, and Salwarpe (with notices of Westwood Park and the Pakington family)', *A.A.S.R.P.* **5**(1), 1859; 161-86. Includes pedigree of Pakington, 12-19th c.
WILLIS-BUND, J.W. 'Social life in Worcestershire in the first quarter of the seventeenth century, illustrated by the Quarter Sessions Records', *A.A.S.R.P.* **23**(2), 1896, 372-91.

Inkberrow
BRADBROOK, W. 'History of the parish of Inkberrow', *A.A.S.R.P.* **26**(2), 1902, 465-507. Includes will abstracts, parish register extracts, etc., etc.
BRADBROOK, W. 'Inkberrow: parochial records of local government in 1657', *A.A.S.R.P.* **30**(1), 1909, 217-30. Extracts from accounts, with some names.

Leigh
SMITH, SAMUEL. 'The parish and church of Leigh', *A.A.S.R.P.* **17**(2), 1884, 286-302. Includes list of incumbents, notes on inscriptions, a few parish register extracts, etc.

Yorkshire
Acomb
BENSON, G. 'Notes on Acomb, York', *A.A.S.R.P.* **38**, 1926, 72-94. Includes pedigrees of Acomb, 16-17th c., Masterman and Barlow, 17-18th c., with list of vicars, notes on monumental inscriptions, etc.

Sheffield
INCE, T.N. 'Constables duties at Sheffield in 1650', *Reliquary* 5, 1864-5, 23-5. Includes extracts from constables' accounts; also notes on Fox family.

York. St. John
BRODE, T.A. 'Old parish account books of St. John the Evangelist, York', *A.A.S.R.P.* 29(1), 1907, 304-22. Extracts 1580-1800, with some names.

York. St. Martin cum Gregory
BENSON, GEORGE. 'Churchwardens' accounts of St. Martin-cum-Gregory, York', *A.A.S.R.P.* 31(1), 1911, 303-18; 31(2), 1912, 613-28. 1560-1754; not a transcript, but includes a few names.

13. OCCUPATIONAL AND OTHER LISTS OF NAMES ETC.

A. GENERAL
BLACK, W. H. 'On the personal names and surnames used in England in the thirteenth century', *J.B.A.A.* 26, 1870, 328-35. Names used in Hartwell and Stone, near Aylesbury, Berkshire.
CLARK, G. T. 'Remarks upon the worthies of Devon', *A.J.* 31, 1874, 126-52. Includes list of biographies in Prince's *Worthies of Devon.*
KERSHAW, S. W. 'Foreign refugee settlements in East Kent', *J.B.A.A.* 40, 1884, 333-50. Includes names of many refugees, 16-18th c.

B. OCCUPATIONAL
A number of articles in the journals covered by this bibliography provide lists of men engaged in specific occupations, goldsmiths and cutlers, printers and clockmakers. These 'occupational lists' are enumerated here, as are a few works listing persons connected with schools, and a few lists of tradesmens tokens.

Almoners
TANNER, LAWRENCE E. 'Lord High Almoners and sub-almoners, 1100-1957', *J.B.A.A.* 3rd series, 21, 1958, 72-83. List with brief biographical notes.

Armourers
DILLON, HAROLD. 'Armourers and cutlers in 1537', *Reliquary* 3, 1889, 129-32. Includes list of members of two London companies.

Bellfounders
BENSON, GEORGE. 'York bell founders', *A.A.S.R.P.* 27(2), 1904, 623-49. Includes list; 14-18th c.
HOPE, R. C. 'English bellfounders, 1150-1893', *A.J.* 50, 1993, 150-75. List of names.
WALTERS, H. B. 'Notes on Worcestershire bell-founders', *A.J.* 63, 1906, 187-97. Includes list.

Carpenters
HARVEY, JOHN H. 'The King's chief carpenters', *J.B.A.A.* 3rd series, 11, 1948, 13-34. List, 11-16th c., with biographical notes.

Clockmakers
COOPER, T.P. 'The old clockmakers and watchmakers of York', *A.A.S.R.P.* 30(1), 1909, 243-60. Includes list.
MORGAN, C. OCTAVIUS. 'List of members of the Clockmakers' Company of London, from the period of their incorporation in 1631 to the year 1732', *A.J.* 40, 1883, 193-214.

Cutlers
LEADER, J.D. 'Notes on the Cutlers' Company's accounts', *A.A.S.R.P.* 12(2), 1874, 287-300. Sheffield; gives many names, 17-18th c.
See also Armourers.

Goldsmiths
HOPE, R.C. 'English goldsmiths', *Reliquary* N.S. 2, 1888, 216-23; 3, 1889, 31-40, 74-88, 159-67 & 241-5; 4, 1890, 24-34. In London, York, Norwich, Exeter, Newcastle on Tyne and Chester.
PRIOR, MATTHEW. 'The goldsmiths halls in the provinces in 1773', *Reliquary* N.S. 7, 1893, 21-7. Includes list of Chester and Newcastle on Tyne goldsmiths, with Exeter assay office accounts, giving names.
SITWELL, H. D. W. 'The Jewel House and the royal goldsmiths', *A.J.* 117, 1960, 131-55. Includes lists, 16-19th c.

Masons
GEE, E. A. 'Oxford masons, 1370-1530', *A.J.* 109, 1952, 54-131. List with biographical notes.

HARVEY, JOHN. 'The masons of Westminster Abbey', *A.J.* **113**, 1956, 82-101. Includes list, 1341-1534.

Merchants
BOND, EDWARD A. 'Extracts from the liberate rolls, relative to loans supplied by Italian merchants to the Kings of England in the 13th and 14th centuries', *Arch.* **28**, 1840, 207-326. Includes many merchants' names.

Pawnbrokers
PRICE, F. G. HILTON. 'Some notes upon the signs of the pawnbrokers in London in the seventeenth and eighteenth centuries', *A.J.* **59**, 1902, 160-200. Includes list of pawnbrokers.

Pewterers
'London pewterers in 1669', *Reliquary* N.S. **6**, 1892, 50-51. List of prominent members of the trade.
'Old English pewter, IV', *Reliquary* N.S. **7**, 1893, 202-7. Includes list of apprentices at York, 1645-1749.

Pipemakers
ATKINSON, DAVID, & OSWALD, ADRIAN. 'London clay tobacco pipes', *J.B.A.A.* 3rd series, **32**, 1969, 171-227. Includes lists of makers, 17-19th c.
OSWALD, ADRIAN. 'The archaeology and economic history of English clay tobacco pipes', *J.B.A.A.* 3rd series, **22**, 1959, 40-102. Includes 48 page list of pipe makers, showing places and dates; with bibliography.

Potters
JEWITT, LLEWELLYN. 'On a mug of Nottingham ware', *Reliquary* **16**, 1875-6, 65-7. Includes names of potters in Nottingham, 1774 and 1802.

Printers
BURTON, J.R. 'Early Worcestershire printers and books', *A.A.S.R.P.* **24**(1), 1897, 197-213.

Schoolmasters
GUEST, JOHN. 'Provosts of Rotheram College', *Reliquary* **17**, 1876-7, 3-9. List of schoolmasters, 15-16th c., includes will of William Rawson, 1495.
NORTH, THOMAS. 'The ancient schools of Melton Mowbray', *A.A.S.R.P.* **10**(1), 1869, 129-45. Leicestershire; includes list of masters of Melton Grammar School, 1571-1791, with other names.

Sergeants at Arms
SITWELL, H. D. W. 'Royal Sergeants-at-Arms, and the royal maces', *Arch.* **120**, 1969, 203-50. Includes list, 15-20th c.

Students
'St. Peters, York, school register', *N.G.* **2**, 1896, 18-21, 79-82, 139-42 & 160-63; **3**, 1900, 13-16 & 67-71. 1828-44 only.

Swan owners
TICEHURST, N.F. 'The swan marks of Lincolnshire', *A.A.S.R.P.* **42**(1), 1936, 59-141. List of swan owners, 15-17th c.

Tradesmen
CUMING, H. SYER. 'Old traders' signs in Duck Lane', *J.B.A.A.* **49**, 1893, 117-9. Includes names, 17-18th c., as do the following works.
CUMING, H. SYER. 'Old traders' signs in Little Britain', *J.B.A.A.* **49**, 1893, 108-16. 17-18th c.
CUMING, H. SYER. 'Traders' signs on Old London Bridge', *J.B.A.A.* **43**, 1887, 162-73. 16-18th c.
CUMING, H. SYER. 'The old traders' signs in Paternoster Row', *J.B.A.A.* **41**, 1885, 278-83. 16-18th c.
CUMING, H. SYER. 'On the old traders' signs in St. Paul's Churchyard', *J.B.A.A.* **39**, 1883, 241-54. 16-18th c.
CUMING, H. SYER. 'The old traders' signs in Westminster Hall', *J.B.A.A.* **42**, 1886, 137-42.
JEWITT, LLEWELLYN. 'The traders' tokens of Derbyshire, described and illustrated', *Reliquary* **4**, 1863-4, 11-22, 97-107, 162-9, 241-8; **5**, 1864-5, 31-8, 105-12 & 198-200; **6**, 1865-6, 100-8; **7**, 1866-7, 152-61 & 241-9. Includes names of many traders, with much genealogical information. A pedigree of Bateman and Hartington is included in v.6., of Blythe of Norton and Birchet in v.5., of Bower of Winster, Booth of Wirksworth, Kemp of Wirksworth, and Wigley of Wirksworth in v.7.
NORTH, THOMAS. 'Tradesmens tokens issued in Leicestershire in the seventeenth century', *A.A.S.R.P.* **4**(1), 1857, 177-92. Includes genealogical notes.

Author Index

Place Index

Family Name Index